DOUG FRENCH'S VERBAL PREP for the ACCUPLACER®

Doug French

Research & Education

Visit our website at: w

D1119500

Research & Education Association
61 Ethel Road West
Piscataway, New Jersey 08854
Email: info@rea.com

DOUG FRENCH's
Verbal Prep for the Accuplacer®

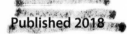

Published 2018

Printed in the United States of America

Library of Congress Control Number 2011922083

ISBN-13: 978-0-7386-0965-2
ISBN-10: 0-7386-0965-X

Cover image: rubberball/Getty Images

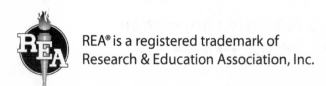

REA® is a registered trademark of
Research & Education Association, Inc.

TABLE OF CONTENTS

DEDICATION

To my sons, for whom I hope the SAT will be abolished by the time they're 16.

ABOUT THE AUTHOR

Doug French has worked in test-preparation since he first signed on with The Princeton Review in 1992. He has worked as an author, instructor, and course developer for the SAT, SAT Subject Tests, LSAT, GMAT, GRE, and way too many other standardized oppressions, until he became a full-time teacher, with summers off and everything, in 2004. He now works as a freelance writer in New York City.

ACKNOWLEDGMENTS

In addition to our author, we would like to thank Larry B. Kling, Vice President, Editorial, for his overall direction; Pam Weston, Publisher, for setting the quality standards for production integrity and managing the publication to completion; Alice Leonard, Senior Editor, for project management; Diane Goldschmidt, Managing Editor, for editorial contributions; and Kathy Caratozzolo of Caragraphics, for typesetting the book. Back-cover photo of author by Karen Walrond.

A special thank-you to Dr. Rena Grasso, for her contribution to our appendix on *Writing Skills and Knowledge.*

ABOUT REA

Founded in 1959, Research & Education Association (REA) is dedicated to publishing the finest and most effective educational materials—including study guides and test preps—for students of all ages.

Today, REA's wide-ranging catalog is a leading resource for students, teachers, and other professionals. Visit *www.rea.com* to see a complete listing of all our titles.

INTRODUCTION

"*If you're used to stressing about standardized tests, you can stop now. The Accuplacer is a totally different type of test, because it's untimed and unscored!*"

Welcome to *Doug French's Verbal Prep for the Accuplacer*, the definitive prep book for All Things Verbal on the Accuplacer. This book is set up to guide you through the test's format, increase your appreciation of English grammar, help you improve your reading comprehension skills, and review the best techniques for writing a good essay. It will also teach you a few tried-and-true techniques that are always helpful on any test that includes answer choices, as this one does.

First, let's start with the basics. Like what the Accuplacer actually is.

WHAT IS THE ACCUPLACER?

The Accuplacer is a test developed by the College Board that is designed to help you assess your ability to work math problems, understand English grammar, and comprehend short reading passages. It's meant to help your academic advisors analyze your academic strengths and weaknesses and "place" you "accurately" in the courses that will be the best fit for you.

Unlike most of the other standardized tests you might encounter, there are two very important aspects of the Accuplacer that you'll probably really like.

- You don't have to worry about getting a certain score, because the Accuplacer doesn't give you one. It's only meant as an assessment, which means you cannot "pass" or "fail" it. You merely want to represent your academic skills as accurately as possible.

- You don't have to worry about time pressure, because the Accuplacer doesn't have a time limit. This test is more concerned with determining what you know, not how fast you can tell people about it. But, doing well on the Accuplacer will help you financially. You will move more quickly through the regular college courses instead of taking non-credit review classes.

Basically, this test is a lot less stressful than most other standardized tests. And that's a good thing, because when you take it you can concentrate on the one question sitting on your computer screen without having to worry about how much time you have left to finish all of them.

And yes, we did say "computer screen," because the Accuplacer is a "computer-adaptive test," sometimes referred to as a CAT.

What is a "computer-adaptive" test?

The Accuplacer is a computer-based exam, so you won't have to bother with paper test booklets and bubble sheets. Instead, the test "adapts" to the level of ability it perceives, based on the questions you've already answered.

When a section begins, the first question you'll see will be of "medium" difficulty. If you get it right, the next question you'll see will be a little "harder"; if you get it wrong, the next question will be a little "easier." And please note that those words are in quotes for a reason: The Accuplacer might have an idea of what makes a question easy or difficult, but that doesn't mean that its perception of difficulty is the same as yours. Everyone is different, and what you think is easy might strike someone else as really hard. Or vice versa.

The bottom line? It's doesn't make a whole lot of sense to worry about whether a question is easy, or difficult, or anywhere in between. Just concentrate on the question you see on the screen, do your best with it, and move on.

Adjusting to the CAT

A good thing about paper-and-pencil exams is that you can work on whatever problem you want to within a given section. If you're not sure how to answer the first question, for example, you can skip it and go to the next one.

On the CAT, however, this isn't an option. The computer gives you a question, and you have to answer it before moving on. You can't scroll ahead to look at the next answer, and you can't go back to check anything you've already answered. You also can't cross off answers in your test booklet (we'll talk more about that later), and you have to use separate scratch paper (which is more of an issue on math problems than for verbal ones).

The test format

The verbal portion of the Accuplacer consists of 40 questions divided into four categories, 10 questions each. The first two sections are all about sentence skills; the third and fourth are about reading comprehension.

- Part I: Decide whether the sentence structure (grammar, word order, and punctuation) is correct and, if not, select the best way to fix it.

- Part II: Rewrite a given sentence using a different word structure while keeping the same meaning as the original sentence.

- Part III: Read a short passage (5-6 sentences) and answer a question about it.

- Part IV: Determine the relationship between two sentences.

If the description of these questions seems a little vague right now, don't worry. You'll see plenty of examples of each in this book.

The verbal portion of the Accuplacer also contains a WritePlacer test that measures your ability to write effectively. The assignment will be to write a multi-paragraph essay of 300–500 words on the topic provided.

You can also find out more information about the test on the College Board's Accuplacer website: www.collegeboard.org/student/testing/accuplacer.

How to use this book

This book devotes a chapter to each of the four categories described above. Each chapter lists some basic concepts of the Accuplacer tests and offers several drills to help you improve your skill set. In chapter 1, for example, there is a section on each of the grammar issues that the Accuplacer routinely tests, as well as references to the grammar and idiom glossaries, which appear at the end of the book. In chapter 3, on reading comprehension, we'll offer you some techniques for processing written information more quickly and efficiently.

At the end of the book are two 40-question practice tests, each with an annotated answer key. As you work on these questions, as well as the others interspersed throughout the chapters, look for patterns in the questions you answer correctly and those that you keep getting wrong. This will help you pinpoint your strengths and weaknesses and guide you to the areas in which you need the most practice.

And throughout the book, we will endeavor to take advantage of the Accuplacer's most glaring vulnerability: the answer choices.

POE shall set you free

Since every question you'll see on the Accuplacer will have four answer choices, one of the most useful skills you'll develop as you study is the ability to determine why an answer choice is *wrong*. And that's where the Process of Elimination (POE) comes in. The Accuplacer's writers have a very specific task: to write a question and supply an answer to that question. That's the easy part. The hard part is writing the wrong answers—the "decoys"—that can seem attractive enough to choose.

For example, let's look at a sentence that appears on the first page of this introduction:

"Unlike most of the other standardized tests you might encounter, there are two very important aspects of the Accuplacer that you'll probably really like."

Now let's re-envision it as the given sentence in a question in Part I of the Accuplacer and throw in some answer choices:

Unlike most of the other standardized tests you might encounter, <u>there are two very important aspects of the Accuplacer that you'll probably really like.</u>

A. there are two very important aspects of the Accuplacer that you'll probably really like.

B. there are two of the Accuplacer's aspects that are very important and you'll probably really like them.

C. the Accuplacer has two very important aspects that you'll probably really like.

D. the Accuplacer's two very important aspects will very probably be liked by you.

You may not have picked up on this when you first read it, but the sentence is written incorrectly. It begins with the phrase *Unlike most of the other standardized tests you might encounter*, which is a descriptive phrase, or a modifier. When a sentence begins in this way, the noun that follows right after the comma must be the subject that the opening phrase modifies.

- Answer choice (A), which is always a repeat of the sentence as written, violates this rule. So you can cross it out.

- Answer choice (B) has a similar problem, and it creates a run-on sentence at the end. So cross that one out, too.

- Answer choice (D) seems to address the modifying problem, but it also contains the passive voice "liked by you" at the end. Out it goes.

You're left with answer choice (C), which is the credited answer. The opening phrase describes "the Accuplacer," which is *unlike most of the other standardized tests you might encounter*. So the first words that appear in the underlined portion of the sentence must be *the Accuplacer*.

The point of all this is that even if you didn't know about the Misplaced Modifier Rule (which we'll discuss at great length in the next chapter), you can select the credited response either by recognizing what's right about the best one or by recognizing what's wrong about the wrong ones.

If you're down to two

In many cases, you'll be able to get rid of two answer choices rather easily, but you'll find yourself having a tough time deciding between the final two choices. In this circumstance, most of our minds are wired to think in terms of positivity, and to find the answer choice that is defensibly better than the other. That's all fine and wonderful in real life, but in the hardscrabble world of standardized testing, the opposite is true. When you're sizing up two answer choices and playing them off each other, it's actually much easier to point out why the wrong answer is wrong than it is to defend why the best answer is the credited response. So you'll actually make things easier for yourself if you learn to spot flaws.

Don't look for perfection

Did you also notice that the previous paragraph referred to the "best" answer rather than the "right" answer? This is an important point. When you're trying to choose among the four answer choices, you might not agree with what the test deems the "credited response." In fact, many times the credited response is defended not by saying what is correct about it, but by showing the errors in the other answer choices.

The credited response might not be perfect, but it will always be better than the other three. So when you work on questions, remember that, in some circumstances, you may end up choosing the answer choice that stinks the least.

A word about vocabulary

The Accuplacer does not specifically test your vocabulary by making you define ten-dollar words like *perambulate* (which is a fancier version of walk). However, having a good vocabulary couldn't hurt your chances. When you're reviewing a reading comprehension passage, for example, it will definitely help your comprehension if you know what every word means.

More importantly, a good vocabulary will come in very handy when you're writing your essay, because any writing benefits from 1) word variety and 2) a good command of using the right word at the right time.

If you don't think you have the strongest vocabulary in the world, there's no need to stay up nights reading a thesaurus. Instead, you can make a daily exercise of improving your vocabulary by reading as much as you can, either for school or for pleasure, and taking note of any word whose meaning you don't know. If you're not sure whether you know the word's meaning, ask yourself if you'd feel comfortable using it in a school essay.

If not, use a 3 x 5 note card and make a flash card with the word on the front and the meaning on the back. If you really want to get word nerdy, you can annotate it in any way that helps you remember the word's meaning:

- list some synonyms, like *loquacious* and *garrulous*

- include the etymology, or the word roots, and see if they relate to any other language you've studied (especially Latin)

- take note of prefixes or suffixes (like *circum-* means "around" in *circumnavigate*)

- think up a mnemonic device, and the wackier it is, the more likely you'll remember it

Once you start amassing a large stack of these flash cards, start studying and separate them into KNOW and DON'T KNOW piles. And don't try to study a huge batch of words all at once. Take 5–10 of them at a time and work with them over and over until you know them.

Now that we've covered some basic elements, let's get to it. Keep practicing, stay focused, and good luck!

CHAPTER 1: *Correcting Sentences*

"Mastering grammar on the Accuplacer is less challenging than you think, because it tests the same rules over and over again."

The first ten questions you'll see on Part I of the verbal portion of the Accuplacer will be sentences that may, or may not, need correcting. If you read the introduction (and if you haven't, you should), you saw that each of these questions consists of one sentence—part of which has been underlined—and four answer choices:

Padma chose <u>the bigger of the</u> seven cupcakes.

    A. the bigger of the

    B. the biggest than

    C. the biggest of the

    D. bigger than the

If you think the sentence is written correctly, choose answer choice (A), which always repeats the underlined portion word for word. If you see a flaw in the sentence, however, you can cross off answer choice (A) and look for something better among the remaining three choices, which suggest alternative ways to write the sentence.

What not to do

When you see a question like this, your first instinct might be to re-read the sentence four times, with each of the four answer choices included in the underlined portion. If you do this, be aware that the sentences might start to sound unnervingly alike, and your job might actually become more difficult.

A second instinct might be to re-write the sentence in your head and then look for a match among the answer choices. This might seem like the best way to go, but it can cause more problems than you might think. If a sentence is written incorrectly, there is always more than one way to fix it. If you decide on one specific remedy, and it's not there among the last three choices, you might be inclined to pick the one closest to what you want it to be, and that might not necessarily be the credited response. As always, the key lies in a deeper appreciation of grammar and strategy.

The big three for POE

When attempting to correct a sentence, here are the three best strategies to consider:

1. Spot a problem with the sentence as written.

2. Eliminate all the other answer choices that repeat the same problem.

3. See where the answer choices are different from each other and decide which of them is/are flawed.

Let's use these techniques on that sample question we saw earlier in the chapter:

Padma chose the bigger of the seven cupcakes.

    A. the bigger of the

    B. the biggest than

    C. the biggest of the

    D. bigger than the

The most efficient way to go after this question is to recognize that, since it specifically mentions *seven cupcakes*, it's incorrect to use *bigger*. Words that end in –*er* are comparatives that are used when only two things are being compared. When a sentence refers to three or more items, the proper term to use is a superlative, which ends in *–est*. We can therefore eliminate answer choice (A), which we know is incorrect, and answer choice (D), which repeats the error.

There's an example of Steps 1 and 2 in use right there. Since you know *biggest* is the right word, the next step is to compare the other parts of answer choices (B) and (C). How are they different?

Answer choice (C) keeps *of the* after *biggest*, but since answer choice (B) unnecessarily changes *of the* to *than*, you can cross it off. The only answer left is the best answer, choice (C).

Look for a two-and-two split

While looking at the answer choices, you'll often see that the four options often split off into two camps. In this case, it was *bigger* or *biggest*. This can be a helpful trend to recognize. If you didn't know or recognize this rule (and you should, because the Accuplacer frequently brings it up), you have to try something else because you can't just skip ahead to the next question. In this circumstance, you might consider bypassing Steps 1 and 2 and looking at how all four answer choices differ from each other. Since two of them include *bigger*, and the other two include *biggest*, you could conclude that using *bigger* or *biggest* is an important issue. And now it's time to make an educated guess as to which two answer choices to eliminate.

Reminder: Don't look for perfection

As we mentioned in the introduction, it's important to remember that the credited response might not match what you think the answer should be. This is especially true when you're correcting sentences. When you're trying to choose among the four answer choices, you might recognize that the sentence is incorrectly written and cross off answer choice (A). You might also think you have a good idea about how to correct the sentence and look among the remaining answer choices for a match. Unfortunately, if that match isn't there, you might feel frustrated and choose an answer just because it's closest to what you want the credited response to be.

If none of the four answer choices seems "correct," remind yourself that one of them has to be the credited response, which means it has to be defensibly better than the other three choices. Alter your expectations, consider the merit of each answer choice individually.

Keep these techniques in mind as you work through the drills and practice questions in this and other chapters, and you may find yourself spotting trends and wrong answers much more quickly and easily. And now, on to the grammar!

Reviewing the basics

As we prepare to review some of the standard rules of English grammar, it's important to note that this book will not cover every rule known to man. There are plenty of textbooks (some of which you might still have somewhere in the back of your closet) that will teach you all about diagramming sentences. Our goal is to give you a basic overview and prepare you for the errors that the College Board usually wants you to find. We'll also define a lot of grammar terms, so you can tell the difference between a "past participle" and the "present perfect." And if you forget anything, all the definitions appear in the Appendix on page 189.

The simple sentence

The only things a correctly formed sentence really needs are a **subject** and a **verb**. The subject commits the action that the verb describes:

Joe ran.

After that, everything else is just adding detail by adding more description. For example, we can add an **adverb** to describe how he ran:

Joe ran quickly.

From there, we can add a **prepositional phrase** to tell where he ran:

Joe ran quickly down the field.

Why was Joe running?

Attempting to score the winning touchdown, Joe ran quickly down the field.

Before you know it, you've got a more complex sentence that tells you a lot more about what Joe is doing, and where he's doing it. Regardless of all that, however, you can still boil the sentence down to the subject and verb, the most basic elements.

THE MOST COMMON MISCUES

So far, the idea of having to memorize all these grammar rules might be making you dizzy. And that's to be expected. The good news is that even though it's a good idea to review all these rules, there are several that the College Board likes to test over and over again. Therefore, here's a list of the six most common error areas that the Accuplacer wants you to recognize. Each section comes with tips on how to spot them and fix them, as well as several sample questions on which to practice your newfound expertise.

1. Misplaced modifiers

There is one basic rule about words or phrases that describe or modify other words: In a properly constructed sentence, modifiers should appear next to the word or words they describe. If not, then the modifier is *misplaced*. Your job is to determine if the modifier is properly placed in a sentence and, if not, choose the answer that fixes the error.

How to spot modifier errors: The most common structure is a descriptive phrase set off by a comma at the beginning of a sentence, like this: "Like Arizona, it gets really hot in Texas during the summer." This sentence is written incorrectly, because the opening phrase "Like Arizona" is supposed to describe Texas.

How to fix them: The most common way is to make sure the first word after the comma is the word that the opening phrase describes: "Like Arizona, *Texas* gets really hot in the summer." Another way, however, is to turn the opening phrase into a clause, which means rewrite it with a subject and verb. For example:

INCORRECT: While crossing the street, a car ran a red light.

CORRECT: While *I was* crossing the street, a car ran a red light.

Now that the opening is a clause, the sentence is fine.

> **DRILL #1** *Indicate whether the following sentences are written correctly. If not, re-write them to correct the misplaced modifier.*

1. While baiting his hook, a fish jumped into Bob's rowboat.

2. Steeped in a tradition of success, the New York Yankees have won more World Series championships than any other team.

3. First published in 1859 in 32 weekly installments, many literary experts believe *A Tale of Two Cities* to be Charles Dickens's best work.

4. Though usually a calm person, Albert's patience could not withstand the heavy traffic.

5. Unlike dogs, which are much more social, cats tend to keep to themselves.

The answers are on page 35.

2. Restrictive and Non-restrictive modifiers

This section refers to one of the Accuplacer's most niggling details, and it involves how nouns are modified. If a modifying phrase or clause is essential to the sentence because it gives important information that identifies the subject, it is called a **restrictive modifier**. Unlike the modifiers discussed above, restrictive modifiers are not preceded by a comma. Here's an example of the difference:

My son who went to law school just ran a marathon.

The absence of commas in this sentence tells the reader that the speaker has more than one son, and the phrase "who went to law school" is the essential to distinguish the son in the sentence from the other sons. When commas are added, however, the sentence takes on a new meaning:

My son, who went to law school, just ran a marathon.

In this sentence, the commas indicate that the speaker has just one son, so it's no longer necessary to set him apart from the others. Therefore, the modifying phrase now provides extra information that isn't as important as before. This sort of phrase is also called an **appositive**.

Deciding between which of the two structures is correct can be tricky, but you'll get the hang of it with more practice. The main point is to remember that the Accuplacer could deem either structure as a credited response.

DRILL #2 ▶ *Indicate whether the following sentences are written correctly (in these cases, we've included underlined portions). If they are not, re-write them to correct the problem with restrictive or non-restrictive modifiers.*

1. My sister who is allergic <u>to shellfish opened</u> a seafood restaurant.

2. My sister Ellen, who is allergic <u>to shellfish opened</u> a seafood restaurant.

3. The <u>airplane, which was delayed</u> by rain is finally ready for take-off.

4. The majority of <u>puppies, which were born in</u> that shelter have been adopted.

5. The majority of puppies, which are unable to see for the first six weeks of <u>their lives, have been paper-trained</u>.

The answers are on page 36.

3. Pronouns

Pronouns are essential to our conversation, because without them you'd see lots of sentences like this:

> *"When Miles brought Miles's cat to Miles's mother's house, and Miles's mother told Miles that Miles's mother's cat allergy gave Miles's mother a rash on Miles's mother's leg, Miles's mother asked Miles not to bring the cat to Miles's mother's house anymore."*

Instead, we get to shorten sentences so they look like this:

> *"When Miles brought **his** cat to **his** mother's house, and **she** told **him** that **her** cat allergy gave **her** a rash on **her** leg, **she** asked **him** not to bring **it** to **her** house anymore."*

How to spot pronoun errors: Look for pronouns in the underlined portion of a sentence.

How to fix them: Make sure the sentence follows two simple rules.

Every pronoun needs to agree with its antecedent.
A pronoun's antecedent is the noun the pronoun is replacing. A singular noun must be replaced with a singular pronoun, and a plural noun must be replaced with a plural pronoun. Some pronoun disagreements, such as this one, are easy to spot:

> **INCORRECT:** All pronouns must agree with the noun it replaces.

> **CORRECT:** All pronouns must agree with the *nouns they* replace.

The sentences get a little sneakier, however, when certain pronouns are used incorrectly:

> **INCORRECT:** Everyone over 50 needs to review their retirement plan regularly.

> **CORRECT:** Everyone over 50 needs to review *his or her* retirement plan regularly.

The error in the above sentence is rather common in conversation, but it's grammatically incorrect because the subject, *Everyone*, is a singular pronoun. So are *every, each, either, neither, which*, and *none*. You'll see more of this in the subject-verb section of this chapter.

Every pronoun needs to refer directly and unambiguously to its antecedent.
When you write a sentence with pronouns, there is no room for assumption. Whenever the reader encounters a pronoun in a sentence, he or she must know exactly what noun the pronoun has replaced.

>   **INCORRECT:** When Tim and Tony went to town, he stopped off to get some coffee.

In this sentence, we don't know which of the men got coffee because *he* is ambiguous. You can't use a pronoun after the comma; instead, you have to specify which of the men committed the action in the independent clause.

Sentences in the Accuplacer can be particularly ambiguous when two or more pronouns are involved:

>   **INCORRECT:** After Jennifer drove her car into Mary's garage, she tried to take her to court.

This sentence has a big problem, because we don't know who did the suing and who was being sued. We might assume that Mary tried to take Jennifer to court because of the damage Jennifer inflicted, but we don't know that for sure.

Collective nouns
Another tricky consideration on the Accuplacer is when a pronoun replaces a noun that represents a group of people. These are called **collective nouns**, and they're singular.

>   **INCORRECT:** The team finally moved into their new stadium.

>   **CORRECT:** The team finally moved into *its* new stadium.

The subject of the sentence is *team*, which is a singular noun. So the proper pronoun to use is *it*. Note: If the sentence read, "The Yankees finally moved into their new stadium," that would be correct because *Yankees* is a plural noun. Sometimes, however, the construction of a sentence can be deceptive, and you have to keep track of what the subject of the sentence actually is.

INCORRECT: The team of researchers boarded their charter flight to Borneo.

It's easy to think that the subject of the sentence is *researchers*, because they're the ones boarding the plane. However, the subject of the sentence is *team*, and *of researchers* is a prepositional phrase describing what type of team it is. The corrected sentence is: "The team of researchers boarded its charter flight to Borneo."

Subject and object pronouns
Subject pronouns, which perform the action in a sentence, are different from object pronouns, which receive the action. When you're not sure which pronoun to use, refer to this chart:

Subject pronoun	Object pronoun
I	me
you	you
he	him
she	her
it	it
we	us
they	them
who	whom

The pronoun you use depends upon what the word is doing in the sentence:

She gave the ball to him.

In this example, you know that the woman (she) is performing the action, and the man (him) is receiving it. Most sentences on the Accuplacer are this simple, but there are a few sneaky possibilities:

> **INCORRECT:** Between you and I, Cheryl really needs to start studying more.

> **CORRECT:** Between you and *me*, Cheryl really needs to start studying more.

The incorrect construction might seem OK because it's often heard in conversation, but it's not. The key is to separate the two pronouns; *between you* makes sense, but *between I* does not. Here's another structure that is commonly misused:

> **INCORRECT:** She is older than me.

> **CORRECT:** She is older than *I*.

In this sentence, *she* and *I* are being compared, so they both need to be subject pronouns. If this seems confusing, try finishing the sentence by adding a verb, like this:

> She is older than I <u>am</u>.

This sounds much better than the alternative: She is *older* than me am.

Note that *Who vs. Whom* is addressed on the last line of that chart. These pronouns are commonly confused, but their use becomes more simple when you think that *who* is a subject and *whom* is an object. So if the person performing the action is unclear, use *who*:

> *Who left the dirty dishes in the sink?*

If you don't know the identity of the person receiving the action, use *whom*:

> *To whom should I address this letter?*

DRILL #3 > *Indicate whether the following sentences are written correctly. If not, re-write them to correct the pronoun problem.*

1. Georgia and her mother don't know where her violin is.

2. The Department of Sanitation was unable to explain why they took so long to pick up all the garbage.

3. As the corn farmers delivered their crop, they were shocked to learn they were filled with meal worms.

4. The soccer team decided they had practiced enough for one day.

5. None of the doctors were able to diagnose the problem.

The answers are on page 36.

4. Verb tenses

Verb tense is a huge part of the Accuplacer, because there are so many different verb tenses to know about. We'll be listing them here, and in the process we'll be defining a lot of grammar terms. Remember that although you should know the tenses themselves, the Accuplacer won't test whether you know their official grammatical names. We're just defining them here so you'll be able to follow along when they're referred to over and over.

In most cases, the verb tense of a sentence doesn't need to change. Therefore, if you notice that a verb tense isn't consistent throughout a sentence, look to see if that tense shift is really necessary. Also, it pays to look at the part of the sentence that is not underlined, because the verb tense in that portion isn't going to change.

"Every time George goes to the store, <u>he will get a box of Cheerios</u>."

The non-underlined part of the sentence is in the simple present tense, and that sets the tone for the rest of the sentence. Therefore, there's no need to use the future tense *he will get* in the underlined part. The correct sentence reads like this:

*"Every time George goes to the store, he **gets** a box of Cheerios."*

How to spot verb tense errors: Check the tense of the verbs in a sentence and see if they're all in the same tense. If they're not, figure out if the tense shift is necessary.

How to fix them: Use the non-underlined portion of the sentence to figure out what the sentence means to say, and make sure the proper tense is being used to say it. (It might help to put these tenses on flash cards, just so you know when to use which.)

The basic tenses

In a simple sentence, the most common verb tenses are:

- the **past tense**, in which the action happened before:

    *Alice **attended** the University of Oregon.*

- the **present tense**, in which the action is happening now:

    *Alice **attends** the University of Oregon.*

- the **future tense**, in which the action will happen later:

    *Alice **will attend** the University of Oregon.*

You've probably seen these structures many times, so they're relatively easy to recognize (and fix, if necessary).

The complex tenses

There are also three more complicated verb tenses that we'll refer to often in this book, and which you should be able to recognize:

- The **past perfect tense** is used when two things happened in the past, and you want to indicate which of the events came first by using the auxiliary verb *had*:

> Alice **had attended** the University of Oregon for two years when she declared her major.

In this example, we know that Alice attended school for two years before she declared her major.

- The **present perfect tense** uses *has* or *have* to indicate that something began happening in the past and is still happening now:

> Alice **has attended** the University of Oregon since her family moved to Portland.

Now we know that Alice started school in the past, and that she is still there. Note: one of the best clue words to the present perfect is *since*.

- The **future perfect tense** is used to predict when something will end in the future, and it uses *will have*:

> When Alice finishes her doctoral program, she **will have attended** the University of Oregon for seven years.

This sentence predicts that Alice will finish her doctoral program at a specific point in the future.

Other verb tenses

The **conditional** tense usually appears in *if-then* form, such as in this example:

> "**If** I go to bed early, **then** I will not oversleep."

The *if* portion of the sentence happens first, and the *then* portion happens in the future. As a result, the first part of the sentence is usually in the present tense, and the second part uses the auxiliary verb *will* and is in the future tense.

Other phrases to look for in conditional sentences are *provided that* and *on the condition that*, both of which can be substituted for *if*:

> *"I will drive to the beach **provided that** I get my car's brakes fixed."*

> *"My dad let me borrow the car **on the condition that** I finish my homework first."*

If a sentence discusses a general condition or commonly accepted truth, you might see the entire sentence in the present tense, like this:

> *"If my dog starts pacing around in the corner, I **take** him for a walk."*

The **hypothetical** (or imaginary) tense indicates that something is not true, but you're indicating (or imagining) what would happen if it *were* true. And you're not hallucinating, because that last sentence is written correctly because it correctly uses what is called the **subjunctive** mood:

> **INCORRECT:** If I was a rich man, I would buy the Denver Broncos.

> **CORRECT:** If I **were** a rich man, I would buy the Denver Broncos.

To use the subjunctive correctly, always use *were* instead of *was* when describing your own hypothetical situations. *Were* goes in the conditional part of the sentence (the part beginning with *if*), and the verb for the main clause of the sentence is *would*.

DRILL #4 *Indicate whether the following sentences are written correctly. If not, re-write them to correct the problem with the verb tense.*

1. George had been working on his doctoral thesis for almost five years.

2. If I were a foot taller, I would be playing professional basketball.

3. Three months ago, I will have had this car for ten years.

4. If the children behave well, I will let them watch another hour of television.

5. I want to graduate from college next year, but I will not have earned enough credits by then.

The answers are on page 37.

5. Parallel construction

In the same way that verb tenses are usually consistent throughout a sentence, parallel construction dictates that all nouns in a list, as well as all multiple verbs, should be written in the same form.

How to spot parallel construction errors: Look for any list of items set off by commas, or for a sentence in which more than one verb is assigned to one subject. In many cases, part of that list will be underlined, and the rest of it will not.

How to fix them: Consult the non-underlined portion of the sentence, and determine how the underlined (or changeable) portion must be made to agree. And make sure all things that appear in a list are in the same form.

DRILL #5 *Indicate whether the following sentences are written correctly. If not, re-write them to reflect a parallel structure.*

1. Albert's favorite hobbies are playing golf, building bird houses, and to tend to his garden.

2. My father attributes his long life to exercise, a healthy diet, and avoiding stress.

3. After two terms in office, the congressman chose to retire rather than to run for re-election.

4. In my opinion, the best fruits to use in salads are grapefruits, due to their acidity, apples, for their tangy crunch, and avocados.

5. During a job interview, it is important to shake hands firmly and to be maintaining eye contact with your interviewer.

The answers are on page 37.

6. Subject-verb agreement

Even though subject-verb agreement is one of a sentence's most basic needs, the Accuplacer doesn't test it very often. When a subject-verb question does appear on the test, the sentence is often written in a sneaky way, with lots of descriptive words between the subject and the verb, like this:

The albino tiger snake, a species indigenous to the deepest recesses of the Amazon river basin and sought by poachers for its unique skin that is often used to make designer purses and shoes, are now protected under a new wildlife law.

At first, you might think this sentence, though really wordy, is grammatically correct—especially when you note that the nearest noun to the verb *are* is *shoes*. The subject of the sentence, however, isn't *shoes*. It's *snake*, which is singular and therefore does not agree with the plural verb. The corrected sentence looks like this:

The albino tiger snake, a species indigenous to the deepest recesses of the Amazon river basin and sought by poachers for its unique skin that is often used to make designer purses and shoes, *is* now protected under a new wildlife law.

How to spot subject-verb errors: Determine the subject and verb of a sentence, and look for lots of modifiers (adjectives, adverbs, and especially prepositional phrases) that are usually included to distract you. Usually, the subject of the sentence is underlined but the verb is not, or vice versa.

How to fix them: Circle the subject(s) and verb(s) in the sentence and see if they agree with each other.

Pronoun agreement
Remember all that talk in the Pronouns section about singular pronouns? That's an important consideration for subject-verb agreement, because a lot of pronouns are deceptively singular.

> **INCORRECT:** Each of the 50 states have two Senators.

> **CORRECT:** Each of the 50 states **has** two Senators.

In these sentences, *of the 50 states* is a prepositional phrase, and the subject of the sentence is *Each*, which is singular.

If you're ever not sure whether a pronoun is singular, see if you can add the word *one* after it. In this case, it makes grammatical sense:

> *Each **one** of the 50 states has two Senators.*

Other singular pronouns include: *another, any, anything, either, every, everybody, everyone, neither, no one, nobody,* and *none.*

DRILL #6 ▶ *Indicate whether the following sentences are written correctly. If not, re-write them to make the subjects and verbs agree.*

1. Indicate whether each of these questions is written correctly.

2. Of all tropical fish, the blue tetra is one of the least aggressive to divers.

3. A secret trove of gold and doubloons was discovered off the coast of Cape Hatteras.

4. The sea turtle, which many confuse with its terrestrial cousins, are faster and more mobile than you might think.

5. Neither of these women, regardless of her qualifications, are right for this job.

The answers are on page 38.

ODDS AND ENDS

The remainder of this chapter is devoted to grammar rules that the Accuplacer tests less often and don't necessarily fit into any of the categories we've already discussed. Still, they've occurred often enough to be included in this book, and the rules are very clear-cut. So it can't hurt to memorize them.

Negative Inversion

Negative inversion is a sentence format that doesn't show up very often on standardized tests, but the Accuplacer likes to test it. The structure is rather straightforward: A sentence begins with a negative phrase, and the order of the subject and verb are switched, like this:

> **INCORRECT:** Not since 1929 the United States had seen such a threat to its economy.
>
> **CORRECT:** Not since 1929 *had the United States* seen such a threat to its economy.

The sentence starts out with a negative word *Not*, and the subject *the United States* and the auxiliary verb *had* are switched in order.

How to spot negative inversion errors: Look for a negative phrase that starts a sentence. (The structure will be more apparent with more practice.)

How to fix them: Make sure the correct sentence adheres to the formula, where the auxiliary verb is put in front of the subject. POE is usually a great help.

Comparatives vs. superlatives

When you're comparing two things, add **–er** to the end of the adjective to form a **comparative**:

> *Rhode Island is **smaller** than Maine.*

If a sentence compares three or more things, add **–est** to the end of an adjective to form a **superlative**:

> *Rhode Island is easily the **smallest** of all New England states.*

When you can't add **–er** or **–est** to a word, use *more* when you have a comparative sentence, and *most* when the sentence contains a superlative:

> *The United States has **more** people than Canada, but Canada has the **most** miles of shoreline in the Western hemisphere.*

Quantity Words

The word *more* works with things that are countable (like cars) and uncountable (like traffic). The flipside, however, is different. If the nouns are uncountable, you can use *less*:

> *After our baby was born, we had a lot **less** time to socialize.*

If the nouns are countable, however, you have to use *fewer*:

> *After our baby was born, we had **fewer** hours in the day to relax.*

This rule often makes students stumble because *fewer* doesn't come up all that much in regular conversation. If you memorize the rule, though, you'll be fine. The same holds true for *many* (to be used for countable things) and *much* (for uncountable things):

> *There is too **much** traffic in Los Angeles because too **many** people drive to work.*

The last pair of quantity words is *between* and *among*, whose rules are a lot like those for comparatives and superlatives. Use *between* if two things are involved:

> *I can't choose **between** scarlet and burgundy for the color of the new drapes.*

If there are three or more choices, use *among*:

> ***Among** all the essays submitted, Clara's was the most coherent.*

DRILL #7 ▸ *Indicate whether the following sentences are written correctly. If not, identify the error and re-write them.*

1. Never in the history of communication technology has improved so swiftly.

2. We would get to the checkout counter faster if there were less people in front of us.

3. Texas has more oil wells than any other state in America.

4. Yao Ming is the tallest man in the NBA.

5. In a presidential election, voters usually choose among the Democratic candidate and the Republican candidate.

The answers are on page 38.

Run-on sentences

Run-on sentences are one of the Accuplacer's pet peeves, there's usually at least one on every test. And that last sentence, appropriately enough, is an example of a run-on, which is formed when two independent clauses (which could stand on their own as sentences if they had to) are jammed together and separated only by a comma. If a sentence contains two such clauses, they can be connected with a **linking conjunction**:

> *Run-on sentences are one of the Accuplacer's pet peeves, <u>and</u> there's usually at least one on every test.*

Or by a **semi-colon**:

> *Run-on sentences are one of the Accuplacer's pet peeves; there's usually at least one on every test.*

Sentence linkers have a large place on the Accuplacer, which tests several very specific rules. Since the list is rather long, we'll talk about them in Chapter 2.

Punctuation marks

Another common test subject is how to handle quotation marks when a sentence contains **dialogue**. The rule is simple: All punctuation—including commas, exclamation points, and question marks—should be placed **within** the closing quotation mark.

"I left the newspaper in the kitchen," he said.

"Has anyone seen my car keys?" Dan inquired.

"My college just awarded me a full academic scholarship!" she exclaimed.

Note that the verb at the end of the sentence usually indicates what sort of punctuation mark you need. If you see a verb like *exclaimed*, for example, you know you need to use an exclamation mark.

If a sentence quotes something like a book or song by name, there is no need for any punctuation other than quotation marks:

    INCORRECT: I heard that Herman Wouk wrote "War and Remembrance," in less than two years.

    CORRECT: I heard that Herman Wouk wrote "War and Remembrance" in less than two years.

You know this because "War and Remembrance" is a restrictive modifier that provides essential information to the sentence. Without it, we wouldn't know which book Wouk wrote in such a short time.

DRILL #8 *Indicate whether the following sentences are written correctly. If not, identify the problem and re-write them.*

1. The ice cream truck stopped I got a coconut popsicle.

2. "I can't believe you got a new car!" he exclaimed.

3. The bus stopped on the corner, and got out and went to the bank.

4. "You really need to see the dentist", he said.

5. Economics is based on many behavioral factors; it's unwise to discount any of them.

The answers are on page 39.

SAMPLE QUESTIONS

Now that we've run through the majority of the grammar rules you need to know, try working through these sample Error Identification questions. Remember the rules, and the technique of using Process of Elimination to cross off incorrect answer choices. The answers are on page 39.

1. Near the <u>bookstore at the end of the mall, we decided</u> to get some coffee.

   A. bookstore at the end of the mall, we decided

   B. bookstore, at the end of the mall we decided,

   C. bookstore, at the end of the mall, our decision was

   D. bookstore at the end of the mall, we had decided

2. <u>The houses at the end of the street has been</u> deserted for more than 30 years.

    A. houses at the end of the street has been

    B. houses, at the end of the street, had been

    C. houses at the end of the street have been

    D. houses, at the end of the street, had been

3. <u>Who did the President name as</u> the new Secretary of State?

    A. Who did the President name as

    B. Whom did the President name as

    C. Who, the President named, was

    D. Whom the President named as

4. The basic stages of grief include denial, bargaining, and acceptance.

    A. denial, bargaining, and acceptance

    B. denial, to bargain, and then to accept

    C. denying, bargaining, and also accepting

    D. to deny, to bargain, and to accept

5. My brother joined the Marines after he <u>was graduating</u> from high school.

    A. was graduating

    B. had graduated

    C. will have been graduated

    D. had been graduating

6. <u>Not a book has moved me ever more than,</u> "Gone With The Wind."

    A. Not a book has moved me ever more than,

    B. No book moved me ever more than,

    C. Not a book ever moved me more than

    D. No book has ever moved me more than

7. If I walk my dog late at night, I always <u>take</u> a flashlight with me.

    A. take

    B. will take

    C. would take

    D. have taken

8. Many of today's politicians <u>have less qualifications to govern than their prede-cessors did</u>.

    A. have less qualifications to govern than their predecessors did

    B. are less qualified to govern than their predecessors were

    C. have fewer qualifications to be governing than those of their predecessors

    D. have fewer governing qualifications than those predecessors

9. While I was <u>skating, I fell on the ice, luckily</u> no bones were broken.

    A. skating, I fell on the ice, luckily

    B. skating, I fell on the ice. Luckily,

    C. skating I fell on the ice and luckily,

    D. skating I fell on the ice: luckily

10. When I decided my major, <u>I had difficulty choosing among drama and political science</u>.

    A. I had difficulty choosing among drama and political science

    B. it was difficult to choose among drama and political science

    C. choosing between drama and political science was difficult

    D. my difficulty in choosing between drama and political science

The answers to these sample questions are on page 39.

ANSWERS TO DRILLS

Drill #1: Misplaced Modifiers

1. While baiting his hook, Bob saw a fish jump into his rowboat.

2. Correct.

3. First published in 1859 as 32 weekly installments, *A Tale of Two Cities* is believed by many literary experts to be Charles Dickens's best work.

4. Though he was usually a calm person, Albert's patience could not withstand the heavy traffic.

5. Correct.

Drill #2. Restrictive and Non-restrictive Modifiers

1. Correct.

2. My sister Ellen, who is allergic to shellfish, opened a seafood restaurant.

3. The airplane which was delayed by rain is finally ready for take-off.

4. The majority of puppies which were born in that shelter have been adopted.

5. Correct.

Drill #3. Pronouns

1. Georgia and her mother don't know where Georgia's (or her mom's) violin is.

2. The Department of Sanitation was unable to explain why it took so long to pick up all the garbage.

3. As the corn farmers delivered their crop, they were shocked to learn it was filled with meal worms.

4. The soccer players decided they had practiced enough for one day.

5. None of the doctors was able to diagnose the problem.

Drill #4. Verb tenses

1. George *has* been working on his doctoral thesis for almost five years.

2. Correct.

3. Three months *from now*, I will have had this car for ten years.

4. Correct.

5. Correct.

Drill #5. Parallel construction

1. Albert's favorite hobbies are playing golf, building bird houses, and *tending* to his garden.

2. Correct, because *avoiding* is a gerund, or a verb that is treated like a noun after the suffix *–ing* is added. We'll talk about them more in the next chapter.

3. Correct.

4. Correct.

5. During a job interview, it is important to shake hands firmly and *to maintain* eye contact with your interviewer.

Drill #6. Subject-verb agreement

1. Correct.

2. Correct.

3. Correct.

4. The sea turtle, which many confuse with its terrestrial cousins, *is* faster and more mobile than you might think.

5. Neither of these women, regardless of her qualifications, *is* right for this job.

Drill #7. Negative inversion, comparatives, and superlatives, and quantity words

1. Never in the history of communication *has technology* improved so swiftly.

2. We would get to the counter faster if there were *fewer* people in front of us.

3. Correct, because the sentence compares *Texas* with *any other state*, which is singular.

4. Correct.

5. In a presidential election, voters usually choose *between* the Democratic candidate and the Republican candidate.

Drill #8. Run-on sentences and punctuation marks

1. The ice cream truck stopped, *and* I got a coconut popsicle.

2. Correct.

3. The bus stopped on the corner, and *he (or she)* got out and went to the bank.

4. "You really need to see the dentist," he said.

5. Correct.

ANSWERS TO SAMPLE QUESTIONS

1. The opening phrase *Near the bookstore at the end of the mall* describes where the people were when they decided to get coffee. So the first word after the comma needs to be *we*, and you can eliminate answer choice (C). Also, *at the end of the mall* is a restrictive modifier that tells you where the bookstore was, so there's no need for extra commas. This lets you get rid of (B). (D) is incorrect because it unnecessarily changes the tense of *decided* to the past perfect *had decided*. The best answer is (A).

2. As written, the sentence's subject *houses* and verb *has been* do not agree. So you can eliminate (A), which repeats the error. (B) and (D) are incorrect because they also improperly use the past perfect *had been*. The best answer is (C).

3. This question tests your knowledge of when to use *who* or *whom*. In this case, the unknown person is being chosen, or receiving the action. Therefore, the proper pronoun is *whom*, and you can eliminate answer choices (A) and (C). (D) is incorrect because it is a sentence fragment. The best answer is (B).

4. This question is written correctly, because the three elements are listed using a parallel structure. The closest of the other answer choices to do so is (C), but adding *also* is unnecessary. The best answer is (A).

5. Unlike questions 1 and 2, this question requires the use of the past perfect tense. Two events happened in the past, and one (graduating high school) happened before the other (joining the Marines). Answer choices (A), (C), and (D) use an incorrect tense. The best answer is (B).

6.   This sentence is constructed using negative inversion, and it tests your knowledge of proper punctuation. Since "Gone With The Wind" is a book, and not spoken dialogue, there is no need for a comma in front of it. Therefore, you can eliminate answer choices (A) and (B). You also need to use the present perfect tense, because this book continues to be the one that has moved the author the most. The best answer is (D).

7.   This is a conditional sentence, but it does not describe any sort of imaginary or hypothetical scenario. Instead, it merely states something that happens regularly, and the best tense to use is the present (rather than the subjunctive). The best answer is (A).

8.   This sentence is tricky, because even though there is clearly a two-and-two split between less *than* and *fewer than*, the sentence is corrected in a way you might not have predicted. You know (A) is wrong because *less qualifications* is incorrect. (B) is okay, however, because it does not repeat the error; instead, it changes the plural noun *qualifications* to the adjective *qualified*. Answer choices (C) and (D) are incorrect because they make improper comparisons between *politicians* and *qualifications*. The best answer is (B).

9.   As written, this is a run-on sentence. Therefore, you can eliminate (A); answer choice (C), which repeats the error, is also wrong. Answer choice (D) improperly uses a colon to separate the two clauses, each of which could stand independently. Answer choice (B), the best choice, separates the sentence into two separate sentences.

10.   This is another quantity word issue, and since there are only two choices, *drama* and *political science*, the proper word to use is *between* instead of *among*, and answer choices (A) and (B) can be eliminated. Answer choice (D) is a sentence fragment, so the best answer is (C).

CHAPTER 2: *Rewriting Sentences*

"Show off your newfound grammar skills by creating new sentences based on specific instructions."

On Part II of the Verbal portion of the Accuplacer you will find the second type of question. This type of question involves re-writing sentences. Each problem consists of a correctly written sentence and some instructions as to how to re-write it. The two most common question prompts are:

- The next words will be:

- Your new sentence will include:

Your job will be to identify which of the words (or groups of words) in the four answer choices best answer the question prompt. Here's a sample:

She invested her money shrewdly for years and eventually became a millionaire.

Rewrite, beginning with: <u>Having invested</u>

Your new sentence will include:

    A. it became eventually

    B. yearly money

    C. she eventually became

    D. eventually becoming

The original sentence is written correctly, with the subject *She* and the two verbs *invested* and *became*. Now try to re-write the sentence beginning with *Having invested*:

What form did your new sentence take? Did you recognize it as an opening modifier of the subject *She*? The first part of the sentence would be re-written as *Having invested her money shrewdly for years*, which is a phrase that describes *she*. Therefore, *she* must come directly after the comma, and the rest of the sentence reads *she eventually became a millionaire*. The best answer, therefore, is (C).

Keep Chapter 1 in mind

The first lesson from working with this question is that the grammar rules we talked about in Chapter 1 are very much in effect for these questions as well. As you work on them, you're going to want to refer back to that chapter a lot, but in a slightly different way. Whereas in Chapter 1 we spent a lot of time trying to identify errors, this chapter will emphasize how to write a grammatically correct sentence.

There's still POE

Never fear, though, because even though you'll be approaching these sentences differently, you'll still have four answer choices from which to choose. So if you get stuck on a problem (remember—this is a computer-adaptive test that doesn't let you look backward or skip ahead), you'll still be able to use Process Of Elimination to get rid of as many answer choices as possible and make the most educated guess possible.

How to work a problem

Let's take a moment to work through a problem using the combined force of the grammar techniques we've learned and the Process of Elimination:

She will only be able to travel to Cyprus if she receives a special travel visa.

Rewrite, beginning with: <u>Unless she receives a special travel visa,</u>

The next words will be:

    A. travel to Cyprus will be

    B. she will be

    C. she will not be

    D. she will not have been

The original sentence, as we know, is already written correctly. It is a conditional sentence that uses *if* to indicate the hypothesis (the subordinate clause *if she receives a special travel visa*), and then uses the future tense to indicate what will happen if that hypothesis is fulfilled (the main clause *she will be able to travel to Cyprus*). The re-write instructions want you to flip these clauses around and mention the travel visa first.

If you think about it, you could reverse the order of these clauses to reflect the more traditional if-then format, like this:

If she receives a special travel visa, she will be able to travel to Cyprus.

We're on the right track, but we're not done yet. The first word has to change from *If* to *Unless*, so let's make a quick substitution and see what happens:

<u>*Unless*</u> *she receives a special travel visa, she will be able to travel to Cyprus.*

Wait a minute. That doesn't make sense anymore, because *Unless* suggests that if something doesn't happen, then the conclusion will not come true. Therefore, we can eliminate answer choice (B) right away and tweak the sentence one last time:

> <u>*Unless*</u> *she receives a special travel visa, she will* <u>*not*</u> *be able to travel to Cyprus.*

From this new sentence, which is now correct, we can determine that the best answer is (C). We know that answer choice (A) is incorrect because it doesn't start with *she*, and (D) is wrong because it unnecessarily changes the verb tense from future to the future perfect.

Remember, this isn't a timed test like the SAT. When you're considering these sentences, you have all the time in the world (within reason, anyway) to play around with them until you come across a format that is grammatically correct and matches one of the answer choices. So take as much time as you need to feel confident that you've made the right choice. And the more practice you do beforehand, the more confident you'll feel while you're taking the test.

TWO MORE IMPORTANT LESSONS

Before we get to more questions, there are two more topics that were left for this chapter because they come up much more often on Part II questions. The first is the important distinction between **when to use a gerund**, and **when to use a verb in its infinitive form**.

Gerunds and infinitives

A **gerund** is formed by adding the suffix *–ing* to a verb and turning it into a noun. For example, you can add *–ing* to the verb *eat* and create a word that can be used as the subject of a sentence:

> **INCORRECT:** *Eating* fruits and vegetables are a useful way to lower your cholesterol.

> **CORRECT:** *Eating* fruits and vegetables *is* a useful way to lower your cholesterol.

Note that the singular subject of the sentence is *eating*, which matches up with the singular verb *is*. The plural form *are* is incorrect, because the phrase *fruits and vegetables* isn't the subject of the sentence. Instead, the phrase is actually serving as a modifier that tells you what sort of *eating* is *useful*.

The **infinitive** form of a verb involves *to*, as in:

> *My doctor told me **to eat** more fruits and vegetables.*

The Accuplacer likes to test whether a verb should appear in infinitive form or be changed to the gerund form by adding *–ing*. Some verbs, like *decide*, only take the infinitive, like this:

> **INCORRECT:** Jeff decided applying to engineering school.

> **CORRECT:** Jeff decided *to apply* to engineering school.

Some verbs, like *consider*, only work with the gerund form, like this:

> **INCORRECT:** Marla considered to apply to law school.

> **CORRECT:** Marla considered ***applying*** to law school.

And there are a select few verbs, like *start* or *began*, that are happy with either form:

> **CORRECT:** Jose started *reading* the textbook.

> **CORRECT:** Jose started *to read* the textbook.

Consult the lists!

Before we get to some more sample questions, here are two lists of verbs that are followed by gerunds and by infinitives. These are by no means comprehensive, but they're a really good start. While you're training for this test, or in the normal course of your reading (you *are* reading all the time, taking note of grammar rules and beefing up your vocabulary, right?) be sure to add any verbs that don't appear here.

Verbs always followed by gerunds:

admit	appreciate	avoid	can't help	can't stand
contemplate	delay	deny	detest	dislike
enjoy	escape	excuse	finish	give up
have trouble	resist	imagine	involve	justify
keep	mention	miss	not worth	postpone
practice	put off	quit	recommend	resent
risk	save	suggest	think about	tolerate

In addition to these verbs, *how about…?* is also always followed by a gerund.

Another giveaway is any verb that takes the preposition *of*, such as these examples:

- My sister is *tired of* having to get up every morning for skating practice.

- Paulina is *in the habit of* memorizing five vocabulary words each morning.

- Have you ever *thought of* majoring in finance?

Verbs always followed by the infinitive:

afford	agree	aim	appear	arrange
ask	attempt	beg	choose	claim
decide	demand	expect	fail	guarantee
happen	hesitate	hope	learn	long
manage	mean	neglect	offer	omit
pay	plan	prepare	pretend	promise
prove	refuse	seem	swear	tend
threaten	turn out	wait	want	wish

DRILL #1 *Determine if the following sentences use gerunds correctly. If not, re-write them using the infinitive form.*

1. I can't afford paying these credit card bills anymore.

2. With this head cold, I can barely manage getting up in the morning.

3. I detest taking the city bus.

4. How can you justify spending all that money on baseball cards?

5. I don't mind watching your kids while you go to the grocery store.

6. My landlord is threatening evicting my neighbor.

7. Sometimes, I neglect watering my plants.

8. We had to postpone playing the championship game until after final exams were over.

9. I confess to feeling a little jealous of your new job.

10. To attempt diving off that cliff is crazy.

The answers are on page 60.

DRILL #2 ▶ *Determine if the following sentences use infinitives correctly. If not, re-write them using gerunds.*

1. If you have a question, please don't hesitate to ask.

2. After too many failed auditions, I gave up to try to be an actor.

3. People don't plan to fail; instead, they usually fail to plan.

4. My sister promised to meet me at the movie theater after dinner.

5. The two diplomats agreed to curb their countries' nuclear programs.

6. It's time that I learned to type without looking at my fingers.

7. I can't stand to see you so unhappy.

8. She refused to wait any longer for the waiter to bring her the check.

9. She demanded to see the manager immediately.

10. My grandmother longed to visit her ancestral home in Germany.

The answers are on page 61.

Linking words

The second topic that the Accuplacer tests very often in this section is words that link other words and phrases together. The College Board groups these words in three categories, and for that reason we'll discuss them within those groups. Obviously, it's not important to know which words or phrases belong in which category. Rather, the key is to recognize how each of them works correctly in a sentence.

Emphasis linkers

The word *rather* in that last sentence is a good example of the first type of linking word, what we call the **emphasis linker**. These are words that indicate whether a new thought is consistent with the previous one (words such as *furthermore* and *therefore*) or contrary to it (such as *rather* and *however*). These words are often adverbs, such as *obviously* and *conversely*. Here are a few examples:

- **However**, the governor refused to raise taxes.

- **Furthermore**, large colonies of bees are starting to disappear at an alarming rate.

- **Obviously**, it's not important to memorize every single word in the dictionary.

You can also put these words in the middle of a sentence, as long as they are separated by commas. This reflects that the words themselves have no bearing on the structure of the sentence:

- The governor, **however**, refused to raise taxes.

- Large colonies of bees, **furthermore**, are starting to disappear at an alarming rate.

- It's not important, **obviously**, to memorize every single word in the dictionary.

Noun linkers

The second type of linker joins an independent clause with a noun or noun phrase, like this:

The baseball game was canceled due to the oncoming storm.

In this sentence, *The baseball game was canceled* is an independent clause that can stand on its own. In order to add more detail, however, the noun phrase *the oncoming storm* is added, and they're hooked up by *due to*. And once again, it's possible to invert this sentence by beginning with the linking word and noun phrase, and following with a comma, like this:

Due to the oncoming storm, the baseball game was canceled.

Clause linkers

These are the most common type of linker on the Accuplacer, and they function much like conjunctions do. If you want to link two clauses like *He went to the store* and *He was out of milk*, you can link them together with a clause link like *because*:

*He went to the store **because** he was out of milk.*

The Accuplacer calls words like this **subordinators** because a word like *because* turns an independent clause like *He was out of milk*, which can stand on its own, into the subordinate clause *Because he was out of milk*, which cannot. And as usual, you may begin the sentence with the subordinate clause as long as you follow it with a comma, like this:

Because he was out of milk, he went to the store.

Because is one of the most common subordinators that you'll see on the Accuplacer, and here is a list of some others to look out for:

after	although	as	before
even though	if	since	so that
unless	until	when	where
which	while	who/whom	

Get a feel for the grammar

As you'll see, re-writing sentences (which benefits from a more constructive under-standing of how good grammar works) is a bit more intuitive than finding errors (which benefits from the destructive fun of finding fault in bad grammar). The good news, however, is that sentences made with these linkers follow a very strict structure, and you can get a good feel for it by practicing on drills like this one:

DRILL #3   *Use the instructions to re-write the given sentences.*

1. Located above the Arctic Circle, the Norwegian city of Spitsbergen gets only two hours of daylight in winter.

Rewrite, beginning with: <u>Because</u>

2. Barbara will get a bonus if she signs up 20 new clients.

Rewrite, beginning with: <u>Provided</u>

3. Despite his exceptional skills, Warren did not win the Indianapolis 500.

Rewrite, beginning with: <u>Although</u>

4. Mary, he often thought, was the best older sister he could have hoped for.

Rewrite, beginning with: <u>He</u>

5. Because the student was late, she missed the last train home.

Rewrite, beginning with: <u>Because of</u>

The answers are on page 61.

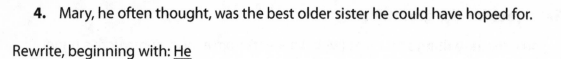 **DRILL #4** *Now try your hand at these sentences, which incorporate the grammar rules we discussed in Chapter 1:*

1. In the event of a tie, the election officials will organize a run-off.

Rewrite, beginning with: <u>If</u>

2. My father had a bad migraine, so he didn't come to the restaurant with us.

Rewrite, beginning with: <u>My father,</u>

3. Delaware is a great state for small businesses because of its relaxed tax structure.

Rewrite, beginning with: <u>Due to</u>

4. Arizona's climate has nurtured several unique plants because it so hot and arid.

Rewrite, beginning with: <u>Hot and arid,</u>

5. The sun went down, and the kids all went home.

Rewrite, beginning with: <u>The kids</u>

6. I am going to run in a race. It is 10 miles long.

Rewrite, beginning with: <u>By the time I finish</u>

7. A domesticated animal would have trouble surviving if left in its own environment.

Rewrite, beginning with: <u>If a domesticated animal were</u>

8. I hadn't seen a seen a bear that large before.

Rewrite, beginning with: <u>Never before</u>

9. Instead of going to the movies, I decided to stay home and read.

Rewrite, beginning with: <u>Rather than</u>

10. If you are over 62 years old, you are eligible to receive Social Security payments.

Rewrite, beginning with: <u>Everyone</u>

The answers are on page 62.

And now, try to incorporate all you've learned with the Process of Elimination to answer these sample questions.

SAMPLE QUESTIONS

1. Norman is a world-class athlete, but his brother struggles to compete in almost every game he plays.

Rewrite, beginning with: <u>Unlike his brother,</u>

Your new sentence will include:

A. whom struggles to

B. who struggles to

C. whose struggle to

D. whose struggles have

2. I fear for the future of humanity on account of the many diseases that we can't seem to cure.

Rewrite, beginning with: <u>Because there is</u>

The next words will be:

A. so much disease

B. so many diseases

C. much of the diseases

D. disease of which

3. The many people who attended the concert finally found their way to the exits.

Rewrite, beginning with: <u>The crowd of</u>

Your sentence will include:

A. found their way

B. found its way

C. were found to

D. was found to

4. After many years of refusals, she finally gave him the pie recipe.

Rewrite, beginning with: <u>He finally received</u>

Your sentence will include:

A. recipe, from

B. recipe, to

C. from her

D. to her

5. After finishing dinner, the boys went upstairs to finish their homework.

Rewrite, beginning with: <u>Once they</u>

The next words will be:

A. had been finished

B. finishing

C. were finishing

D. had finished

6. The extent to which people lavish praise on actors astonishes me.

Rewrite, beginning with: <u>I am astonished</u>

The next words will be:

A. by the extent

B. from the extent

C. of the extent

D. at the extent

7. Carrie Fisher, whose mother was actress Debbie Reynolds, got an early start in show business.

Rewrite, beginning with: <u>Since</u>

Your new sentence will include:

A. because she got

B. because of her

C. her mother was

D. she was

8. The number of cases of tuberculosis seen by doctors decreases each year.

Rewrite, beginning with: <u>Doctors see</u>

The next words will be:

A. less cases

B. less than

C. fewer cases

D. lower than

9. Whereas most American states have some sort of sales tax, Montana has no sales tax whatsoever.

Rewrite, beginning with: <u>Most American states</u>

Your new sentence will include:

A. tax, and Montana

B. tax, but Montana

C. tax unlike Montana

D. tax but Montana

10. I can't play professional basketball because I am not tall enough.

Rewrite, beginning with: <u>If I</u>

The next words will be:

A. were to play

B. was to play

C. was tall enough

D. were tall enough

The answers are on page 63.

ANSWERS TO DRILLS

Drill #1: Gerunds

1. I can't afford *to pay* these credit card bills anymore.

2. With this head cold, I can barely manage *to get* up in the morning.

3. Correct.

4. Correct.

5. Correct.

6. My landlord is threatening *to evict* my neighbor.

7. Sometimes, I neglect *to water* my plants.

8. Correct.

9. I confess feeling a little jealous of your new job.

10. To attempt *to dive* off that cliff is crazy.

Drill #2: Infinitives

1. Correct.

2. After too many failed auditions, I gave up *trying* to be an actor.

3. Correct.

4. Correct.

5. Correct.

6. Correct.

7. I can't stand *seeing* you so unhappy.

8. Correct.

9. Correct.

10. Correct.

Drill #3

1. Because it is located above the Arctic Circle, the Norwegian city of Spitsbergen gets only two hours of daylight in winter.

2. Provided Barbara signs up 20 new clients, she will get a bonus.

3. Although Warren had exceptional skills, he did not win the Indianapolis 500.

4. He often thought that Mary was the best older sister he could have hoped for.

5. Because of the student's lateness, she missed the last train home.

Drill #4

1. If there *is* a tie, the election officials will organize a run-off.

2. My father, who had a bad migraine, didn't come to the restaurant with us.

3. Due to its relaxed tax structure, Delaware is a great state for small businesses.

4. Hot and arid, Arizona's climate has nurtured several unique plants.

5. The kids all went home after the sun went down.

6. By the time I finish the race, I will have run 10 miles.

7. If a domesticated animal were left in its own environment, it would have trouble surviving.

8. Never before had I seen a bear that large.

9. Rather than go to the movies, I decided to stay home and read.

10. Everyone over 62 years old is eligible to receive Social Security payments.

ANSWERS TO SAMPLE QUESTIONS

1. The new sentence is: "Unlike his brother, who struggles to compete in almost every game he plays, Norman is a world-class athlete." This question tests your ability to distinguish *who*, *whom*, and *whose*. You want to keep *struggles* as a verb, but if you use *whose*, then *struggles* becomes a *noun* without a verb and the sentence structure falls apart. Eliminate answer choices (C) and (D). And since you want a subject pronoun to compare with *Norman*, you don't want to use the object pronoun *whom*. The best answer is (B).

2. This is a tricky question, because since the new verb has to be *is*, the plural *diseases* no longer agrees. So you want the singular *disease*, which is not a countable noun and therefore should be modified by *much* instead of *many*. The new sentence is: "Because there is so much disease that we can't seem to cure, I fear for the future of humanity." The best answer is (A).

3. In this case, *The many people* is a plural noun, but *The crowd of people* is singular. Since *crowd* is the noun (and *of people* is the prepositional phrase that modifies it), the proper pronoun is *its*, not *their*. The new sentence is: "The crowd of people who attended the concert finally found *its* way to the exits." The best answer is (B).

4. The new sentence is: "He finally received the pie recipe from her after many years of refusals. There is no need to include a comma after recipe, so you can eliminate answer choices (A) and (B). And since the proper idiom is *received . . . from*, the best answer is (C).

5. The phrase *Once they* requires the past perfect tense, so you need the auxiliary word *had*. Eliminate answer choices (B) and (C). And there is no need to add *been*. The new sentence is: "Once they had finished dinner, the boys went upstairs to finish their homework." The best answer is (D).

6. This question comes down to a simple knowledge of idiom, and *astonished* takes the preposition *by*. The new sentence is: "I am astonished by the extent to which people lavish praise on actors." The best answer is (A).

7. The new sentence is: "Since her mother was actress Debbie Reynolds, Carrie Fisher got an early start in show business." *Because* is redundant, because the sentence already contains *since*. Eliminate answer choices (A) and (B). And answer choice (D) doesn't make sense, because the pronoun in *her mother* refers to Carrie Fisher. The best answer is (C).

8.   This question is a test of your knowledge of quantity words—in this case, *fewer* vs. *less*. There is no reference to another figure to be compared, so there is no need to include *than*. Eliminate answer choices (B) and (D). And since the cases are countable, use *fewer* instead of *less*. The new sentence is: "Doctors see fewer cases of tuberculosis each year." The best answer is (C).

9.   The new sentence is, "Most American states have some sort of sales tax, but Montana has no sales tax whatsoever." It contains two independent clauses that are linked by the preposition *but*, so you need a comma before *but*. Therefore, you can eliminate answer choices (C) and (D). And the two clauses are in opposition to each other, so you don't want to use *and*. The best answer is (B).

10.   This question is a test of the subjunctive mood, because the situation is hypothetical. It reverses the initial idea that he doesn't play ball because he isn't tall enough, and the new sentence asserts that if he were tall enough, he would play. The new sentence is: "If I were tall enough, I would play professional basketball." The best answer is (D).

CHAPTER 3: *Reading Comprehension*

"*It's just like all the other reading comprehension tests you've taken, except now you can take your time and get it right!*"

There are many realities on which you can depend in life, and one of them is that standardized tests include Reading Comprehension questions. There are 10 of them on Part III of the Accuplacer, and when you see them, you might instinctively panic over how little time you have to comprehend them.

But then you might remember that this is the Accuplacer, which has no time limit! So rather than revert to all the skimming techniques you may have learned for other tests, you can take your time, read at your own pace, and consider all of the answer choices carefully without the imposing threat of a ticking clock.

What the questions look like

Each Reading Comprehension question begins with a short paragraph of around 100 words, followed by a question and four answer choices. Here's an example:

In the territory of Wyoming on September 6, 1870, for the first time anywhere in the United States, women went to the polls to cast their ballots. The big surprise was that, after 30 years of political battling on the East Coast, the first victory for a woman's right to vote occurred in Wyoming, where no public speeches, rallies, or conventions for the women's suffrage movement had occurred. Instead, there had been just one remarkable woman: Esther Morris. Her one-woman campaign is a classic example of effective politics. She managed to persuade both rival candidates in a territorial election to promise that, if elected, they would introduce a bill for women's suffrage. She was prescient enough to know that, as long as the winner kept his word, women's suffrage would score a victory in Wyoming.

The author's main purpose is

    A. to analyze political phenomena.

    B. to identify an impediment which Morris experienced.

    C. to emphasize the significance of Morris's achievement.

    D. to denigrate the power of political rallies.

Depending on the difficulty of the question, the text of the passage can be very accessible or a bit dense. The more you practice with them, the more discerning you'll become as you consider which of the provided answer choices is the best.

How to answer them

Obviously, the simplest and most direct way to answer reading comprehension questions is to *read* the paragraph carefully, *comprehend* the subject matter thoroughly, and use the information to choose the best answer to the question provided. And that's what the Accuplacer would have you do, too.

Since there's no time limit, you do have the time to read the passage three, or 20, or 500 times if you want to. (Although it's hard to imagine that you'd want to.) In many cases, the best answer is a close paraphrase of crucial text in the passage.

Know your words!

Recognizing good paraphrases gets much easier if you increase your vocabulary. If you look at that sample question, you can see a lot of top-drawer vocabulary words like *suffrage*, *denigrate*, *impediment*, and *prescient*. The Accuplacer traffics in this level of word-smithery all the time, so the time you spend augmenting your lexicon could have serendipitous ramifications.

Process of elimination

Once again, given the four answer choices that accompany every Reading Comprehension question, it pays to be able to distinguish the good from the not-so-good. Later in this chapter, we'll discuss the three types of questions the Accuplacer likes to use, and the types of answer choices that are the most likely best (and worst) responses to them. But first, let's take a look at that opening question again and run through a sample way to attack it.

The summary sentence

Let's try something. Without doing anything special or relying on any techniques, read the paragraph once, and try to keep your re-reading to a minimum:

> In the territory of Wyoming on September 6, 1870, for the first time anywhere in the United States, women went to the polls to cast their ballots. The big surprise was that, after 30 years of political battling on the East Coast, the first victory for a woman's right to vote occurred in Wyoming, where no public speeches, rallies, or conventions for the women's suffrage movement had occurred. Instead, there had been just one remarkable woman: Esther Morris. Her one-woman campaign is a classic example of effective politics. She managed to persuade both rival candidates in a territorial election to promise that, if elected, they would introduce a bill for women's suffrage. She was prescient enough to know that, as long as the winner kept his word, women's suffrage would score a victory in Wyoming.

And now, without re-reading anything or thinking too much about it, write a sentence below that summarizes what you just read:

How did you do? And how difficult was it? This isn't the sort of thing people do very often, but it can be a good indicator of how much information you can process in a short period of time. Did your summary sentence look anything like this?

The first woman's vote resulted because of one woman, Esther Morris, in Wyoming.

Your summary sentence doesn't have to be supersophisticated or worthy of inclusion in a literary journal. All it should try to do is condense the main idea of the passage and convey the idea that Esther Morris did something that three decades of rallying couldn't accomplish elsewhere. Whatever your sentence looked like, it should have at least included Esther Morris's name, since she's the passage's main character.

Out with the bad

Now, on to the question and answer choices:

The author's main purpose is

> A. to analyze political phenomena.
>
> B. to identify an impediment which Morris experienced.
>
> C. to emphasize the significance of Morris's achievement.
>
> D. to denigrate the power of political rallies.

This is a main idea question the first of the three types of questions we'll discuss later in this chapter, so your main idea sentence can come in handy when you decide which of the answer choices is the best response. You might want to treat this process like dating: if you find one that you like, you can keep it around for a while until something better comes along.

Answer choice (A) has the word *political* in it, and the passage does refer to Morris's accomplishments as something of a phenomenon. But, Morris herself is missing, and the choice is way too general. Eliminate it.

Answer choice (B) mentions Morris, which is good. The key here is in vocabulary, though; an *impediment* is something that blocks your progress, and while you might assume that Morris's efforts had been thwarted previously, there's no specific mention of this in the passage. Instead, the passage is about her success.

Answer choice (C) is the best so far, because it mentions Morris and stresses the magnitude and unlikelihood of her achievement. Keep it.

Answer choice (D) refers to the rallies that seemingly could not effect the change that Morris did, but the passage doesn't say that these rallies never work. And once again, Morris's name is missing, suggesting that this choice is also too wide-open. No good.

Answer choice (C), therefore, is the best response.

TYPES OF QUESTIONS

On the Accuplacer, each question after a Reading Comprehension passage will likely fall in one of three categories: main idea/purpose, specific reference, and inference.

Main idea/purpose questions

Main idea/purpose questions are easily the most common, and they ask you something that relates to the paragraph as a whole. Sample questions look like these:

- The author's primary purpose is

- What is the main idea of this passage?

- This passage is primarily about _____.

A main idea question needs a main idea answer, one that includes just enough detail to sum up what was written. Writing a summary sentence can be useful here, as it will train you to recognize which answer choices have too much or not enough detail. It also helps to look for the thesis statement, which usually explains the passage's main point.

Incorrect choices will usually try to trick you by mentioning something you've read, but it might be too vague or too specific. It also might say something that contradicts the passage entirely.

DRILL #1   *Here are some sample main idea questions. Try to write a summary sentence for each, and then play the answer choices against each other until you find the best one. The answers are on page 83.*

1.   Many criminologists assert that television dramas are affecting the way that court cases are adjudicated. Thanks to several current programs about forensic science, jurors are developing unrealistic expectations of the quality and extent of forensic evidence that can be entered into a court of law. As a result, jurors often suggest using techniques that, although dramatized on television, are either inappropriate for the current case or, in some cases, do not exist. It is up to judges and litigators, therefore, to ground the jurors' expectations in reality.

The main idea of the passage is that

A. forensic science is struggling to keep pace with the public's demands.

B. in many media, art can imitate life, but it can also influence it.

C. jurors often think they have more knowledge of a case than they actually do.

D. the dramatization of crime-scene investigations is influencing the way they are used in real court cases.

2.   For many years, the SAT has been universally acknowledged as the primary test for college candidates to take. Recently, however, the SAT has come under some criticism because of alleged cultural biases, and of the arcane knowledge it predominately tests. As a result, the ACT exam assessment, which many people see as more straightforwardly based on a high school curriculum, is enjoying a new wave of popularity. Students also prefer the ACT's advanced

math and science content, which makes the text more emblematic of the material they are currently studying.

What is the main idea of the passage?

A. The ACT is becoming a more popular alternative to the SAT.

B. The SAT does not take the average high-school curriculum into account.

C. The SAT is rightly criticized for its inherent cultural biases.

D. A student's recall of high-school curricula is the best measure of his or her chances to succeed in college.

3. Each cell in a particular plant starts out with a particular set of genes. The mystery is how these cells know how to form all of the plant's separate structures such as roots, leaves, and fruits. Cellular botanists have recently discovered that these genes are expressed, or "activated," a few at a time through a complex system of hormones and regulatory molecules. This system is comparable to that of many mammals, which have what scientists call a "hormone hierarchy." For example, hormones in the brain are delivered to the pituitary gland, which then releases other hormones to various other parts of the body. It is now believed that plant hormones exist in a similarly tiered system.

The passage is primarily about

A. whether the ultimate role of a plant's cells is predetermined.

B. a similarity between the cellular behavior of plants and animals.

C. important breakthroughs in the field of cellular botany.

D. the opinion that a plant's cellular development is more efficient than a mammal's.

Specific-reference questions

In contrast to main idea/purpose questions, specific-reference questions want you to paraphrase a particular detail in the passage. They will often include *According to the passage* and mention a key word or phrase, which can point you to the place in the passage where the question is answered. These questions are often phrased like this:

- According to the passage, which one of the following statements is correct?

- What is main reason why the cover-up of the Watergate break-in failed?

- According to the passage, the plants and organisms in Antarctica are unique because

You can look at specific-reference questions in an opposite manner to main-idea questions, because many of the wrong answers will be too *general*, and summarize the main idea. Others will be just plain wrong (that is, contradicted by text in the passage).

DRILL #2 *Here are some sample specific reference questions. When you re-read the passage, try to play the answer choices against each other until you find the best one. The answers are on page 84.*

1. Historically, the first company able to bring a new technology to market has used its singular position to establish market share. Subsequent case studies, however, indicate that the dominant position goes not to the originator of the technology, but to the company that establishes the most effective means of mass production and distribution. The Beta format, for example, was the first type of recordable technology available to consumers, but competitors, who created the rival VHS format, used strategic alliances to eclipse Beta within 10 years. Even though Beta had a considerable head start and was no more expensive than VHS, the Beta format had completely vanished by the end of the 1980s.

According to the passage, today's successful companies can earn the greatest profits by

A. being the first to patent a new technology.

B. investing in research to create less-expensive versions of current technology.

C. finding ways to make and deliver its products more efficiently.

D. merging with competitors to create the most dynamic company within an industry.

2. The hexagonal symmetry of snowflakes is as confounding now as it was in the day of Johannes Kepler, one of the first medieval scientists to analyze a phenomenon rather than argue over theories as to its origination. When Kepler observed that all snowflakes were initially formed as perfectly symmetrical six-sided stars, he conjectured that the reason was external, and not molecular. Yet he never managed to understand how spherical droplets of vapor could take on such a singular pattern. Ultimately, he concluded that snowflakes were hexagonal simply because "it is in their nature to be so."

According to the passage, medieval scientists were especially concerned with

A. disputing hypotheses.

B. establishing facts.

C. analyzing phenomena.

D. furthering their reputations.

3. In *Frankenstein*, Mary Shelley depicts two primary characters: one who is perceived as a monster and yet exhibits undeniably human emotions, and the monster's creator, who, though universally respected as a gentleman, sees his unquenchable thirst for knowledge cause him to commit an inhuman act. Some of Shelley's biographers suggest that this literary dualism stemmed from her own difficulties to reconcile contradictory perceptions of herself. Compared to her contemporaries, they assert, the societal pressures exerted upon her as a woman were in constant conflict with her intuitions as an artist.

    The author of the passage mentions *Frankenstein* in order to

    A. assert that perceptions can be deceiving.

    B. identify what would become a popular literary device.

    C. compare the characters Shelley created with her own internal struggle.

    D. emphasize the fine line between heroism and villainy.

Inference questions

The Accuplacer's last common question type is the inference question, which asks you to use the information in the passage to conclude something. To *infer* something means to figure something out without having been specifically told. And if something is indirectly told, it is *implied*. For example, consider these facts:

> *Every day, I go either to school or the library. Today, I didn't go to school.*

From what you read, you can only infer that the narrator went to the library. You might assume he studied there, or checked out some books, because that's what people usually do at libraries. However, you know nothing about what he did there, or how long he stayed, because the passage doesn't give you any information about that. In many cases, answer choices on inference questions can trap you into assuming something that you weren't explicitly told.

Sample questions look like these:

- From this passage, it seems safe to conclude that

- From this passage, we can infer that

- The passage implies which of the following?

Note how they all refer directly to *the passage,* which means the credited response will have nothing to do with any outside knowledge you might have. Rather, it will be supported solely by what you just read. So when you're considering the answer choices, ask yourself: "Based on what I read, do I know that this is true?" Process of Elimination works brilliantly here, because the answer to all of the incorrect answer choices will be "No."

DRILL #3 *Here are some sample inference questions. When you consider each answer choice, ask yourself if you can explicitly defend why it is true, and be careful not to assume. The answers are on page 84.*

1. Genetic researchers have uncovered some unsettling news about the frequency with which bipolar disorder is genetically inherited. Approximately 1 percent of the general population has been diagnosed with some form of bipolar disorder. If one of a child's parents is diagnosed as bipolar, however, that child has a 12 percent chance of suffering from the disease. And the incidence of bipolarism among children of two bipolar parents is a disturbing 45 percent.

   From this passage, it seems safest to conclude that

   A. a person's risk of developing bipolarism is at least partially determined by genetic factors.

   B. incidences of bipolarism are greater among those with one bipolar grandparent than those with no bipolar grandparents.

   C. a child is at greater risk of developing bipolarism if a sibling has the disease.

   D. diagnoses of bipolarism in the general population are increasing by worrisome rates.

2. Rabbits may seem like charming and cuddly pets, but workers in agribusiness hold a decidedly different view. To them, rabbits are ravenous pests whose destruction of crops has only just been quantified. A new study has calculated that each rabbit eats approximately $3 worth of grass and $7 worth of barley per year, a figure that becomes more alarming when one considers that each acre can support as many as 40 rabbits. Wheat farmers suffer most greatly, since each rabbit eats more than $1 worth of the crop each month. And despite farmers' best efforts to curb rabbit reproduction, rabbit populations grow by approximately 2% each year.

The passage implies that rabbits

A. eat more wheat each year than both grass and barley.

B. live in populations that are universally dense.

C. could be exterminated more efficiently if farmers researched more effective means.

D. inflict more monetary damage on wheat crops each year than on grass and barley combined.

3. Multiple sclerosis (MS) attacks the central nervous system by compromising a nerve's protective coating and rendering it unable to transmit electrical impulses. It was widely believed that the disease tricks the body's immune system into attacking these coatings, but the latest findings have suggested otherwise. After analyzing the brains of several patients who had recently died from an MS seizure, neurobiologists saw that although the protective coatings had indeed been impaired, there was no evidence that T cells had inflicted the damage.

Which of the following can be inferred by the passage?

A. Nerves that cannot transmit electrical impulses are biologically dead.

B. The body's immune system is composed at least partially by T cells.

C. A cure for MS can be found in the ability to somehow reconstitute a nerve's protective coatings.

D. The patients in the study could have died from something other than the MS seizure.

Read the question first

Did you notice something about your process when you were trying all of the practice problems in this chapter? After you read the passage, you read the question, glanced at the answer choices, and then … you read the passage again. On a timed section, re-reading like this can seem very wasteful of the precious few minutes you have to work the problem. Even though the Accuplacer has no time limit, you might want to consider reading the question first, so you can consider what you'll have to know about the passage as you read it.

Find your own rhythm

Reading the question first is just one technique that works for some students and not for others. If there's one thing that distinguishes Reading Comprehension questions from all the others, it's that techniques are very subjective. And that's because each person's native ability to read critically is very subjective. Some people have the spectacular (and annoying) ability to read something once and quote it back virtually verbatim. Others need to read something ten times before anything penetrates.

Regardless of your situation, you'll get better with practice, and not just with practice questions. Read more. Read everything. Train your brain to process textual information. Read a newspaper article, then put the paper down (or look away from the computer screen) and ask yourself what you just read. If you take the time to analyze how well you can recall details of something you just read, you'll be able to find the right method to make that process as efficient as possible.

Sample Questions

Try these sample Reading Comprehension questions. Read carefully, and be sure to use the Process of Elimination to get rid of answer choices that can't be right. The answers are on page 85.

1. A recent book about Florence Nightingale tries to undermine her idealized reputation and downplay her contributions to the field of military medicine. The author asserts that Nightingale did not become supervisor of all female nurses until late in the Crimean war, and contributions from nurses during that war were, at best, marginal. In contrast, a new volume of Nightingale's correspondence casts her influence in a much more positive light. The editors cite her crucial role in the creation of the Royal Commission on the Health of the Army, as well as her founding of a nurses' training hospital in London.

   The passage is primarily concerned with

   A. underscoring Florence Nightingale's importance in military nursing.

   B. innovations in the quality of health care in post–Crimean War England.

   C. contrasting approaches to composing a historical biography.

   D. evaluating opposing portrayals of Florence Nightingale's historical import.

2. Currently, institutional investors are prohibited from owning a majority of the shares of a U.S. corporation, or to exert any influence in the way the company is run. Furthermore, any investment entity that owns at least 20 percent of a corporation's stock may not sell those shares without a full day's notice. A sale of that magnitude would cause a panic among the other investors in that company and start a massive sell-off that would cause the stock price to drop precipitously. Having prior knowledge of that sale would give larger investors a considerable advantage over smaller ones who mostly likely would not be aware of the intent to sell.

According to the passage, the purpose of the one-day notice requirement to sell shares is to

A. encourage investors to participate more actively in company decisions.

B. keep owners of the largest shareholders number of shares from unfairly earning short-term profits.

C. suggest that companies benefit when their investors own shares over the longer term.

D. urge smaller investors to watch the corporations they invest in intently.

3. When the Organic Act of 1900 established Hawaii as a United States territory, the new law made an immediate and powerful impact on Hawaiian commerce. Plantation owners could no longer import contract laborers to work their fields, and all previous labor contracts were nullified and had to be completely rene-gotiated. During the first six months after the Organic Act was passed, there were no fewer than 26 strikes and work stoppages, some of which involved immigrant workers of Chinese, Japanese, and Portuguese descent.

The primary focus on the passage is on the

A. inherent flaws of a plantation-based economy.

B. power of unions among Pacific islanders.

C. plight of illegally imported contract laborers.

D. ramifications of a legislative act.

4. Until recently, astronomers believed that the particles in a meteor stream became more dispersed at the edges but remained dense at its center. A new experiment, however, used computer-tracking software to extrapolate the density of hypothetical particles over a period of 5,000 years. And researchers were surprised to learn that, although the edges of the computer-generated stream were indeed dispersed, it was hollow at its center. If this model is accurate, it may explain why Earth often experiences two periods of peak activity during a meteor shower instead of just one.

   From the passage, we can infer that

   A. computer-generated modeling is not yet as reliable as it needs to be.

   B. meteor showers are more random than was originally thought.

   C. the average life span of a meteor shower is 5,000 years.

   D. according to older theories, meteor shower activity always rises to one specific peak and then declines gradually.

5. Most artists think of their art as an attempt to establish a dialogue with the observer. The artist's message cannot exist without someone else to absorb it and, perhaps, offer an alternative view. It is this relationship between separate interpretations of an artist's creation that generates conversations and myriad appreciations of artistic endeavor. Because dialogues require equal effort from both artist and observer, the critic can use his or her body of knowledge to facilitate the exchange of ideas.

   The author of the passage mentions that the role of art critics is to

   A. interpret art in ways a common observer cannot.

   B. help an artist trade ideas with those who view the art.

   C. challenge artists to do their very best work.

   D. save an observer the trouble of viewing a piece of art if it is subpar.

6. Seismologists use the Richter scale to measure an earthquake's magnitude by measuring the energy that the earthquake releases. The levels on the scale are related exponentially, in factors of 32. For example, a quake of magnitude 6 releases 32 times the energy of a quake of magnitude 5, and a staggering 1,024 (or 32^2) times the energy of a quake of magnitude 4. As precise as this scale is, it is not equipped to measure an earthquake's effect on the people and/or buildings above. For this assessment, the modified Mercalli scale is used. The scale ranges from Level I to Level XII, the latter indicating that the surface has incurred catastrophic damage.

    According to the passage, which of the following statements is correct?

    A. The two scales use different criteria to measure earthquakes.

    B. The modified Mercalli scale is more accurate than the Richter scale.

    C. The two scales are often used concurrently for maximum accuracy.

    D. An earthquake that scores highly on one scale will most likely do so on the other.

7. The first photographs were created when a sheet of glass was coated with collodion, a sticky substance containing silver halide crystals that produced metallic silver when exposed to light. Soon, photographers used plastic triacetate, which was more versatile and pliable than glass. Decades later, collodion was replaced by a gelatin that swelled in liquid, and therefore held tightly to the base as the processing chemicals reacted with the silver halides. After the gelatin dried, it shrunk back to normal thickness, creating a shape and position of the image that were more true and undistorted than ever before.

    We can conclude from the information in this passage that collodion

    A. was less durable than gelatin.

    B. was more expensive than gelatin.

    C. contained fewer silver halide crystals than gelatin did.

    D. created a less authentic image than gelatin did.

8. It is common for the human psyche, which is often confounded by the distinction between the world it experiences and the world it wants, to create heroes to reconcile the divide. Heroism feeds on instability and a perceived void, and people cannot resist the seductive allure of a bold figure who will stand up to right wrongs, without regard for fear or personal injury. We humans create these superhuman ideals because they represent all that we find lacking in ourselves, both individually and as a society. And we derive strength from them, hoping they can redeem a flawed universe.

The primary purpose of this passage is to

A. identify inconsistent examples of heroism.

B. discuss the role of heroes in human civilization.

C. dismiss heroism as unnecessary and unrealistic.

D. urge people to act more heroically.

9. Although the federal government requires public elementary schools to begin reading education in kindergarten, many private schools delay reading instruction in favor of basic classes in phonetics and storytelling. Some of these private schools cite studies indicating that early reading is a specific skill not necessarily related to intelligence. And small children who are able to sound out words are not always capable of comprehending the words they recognize. As one educator put it, "Education is not a race."

According to the passage, some private schools believe reading instruction in kindergarten is

A. mandatory.

B. deliberate.

C. premature.

D. vital.

10. The seatbelt is one of the most important safety features ever invented for the automobile. In 1930, an estimated 30,000 people died every year from vehicular accidents. Doctors urged car manufacturers to make the seatbelt standard on all vehicles, as they were on aircraft, and by 1965 all 50 states mandated seat belts for all cars. Inertia causes all objects in a car to move at the same speed as the car itself, creating the illusion that they are one single moving unit. This illusion is shattered when a car comes to an abrupt stop, since each object has its own, separate inertia. Without a seatbelt, a body's forward momentum would send it forward violently, often resulting in serious bodily injury.

All of the following are used to support the author's claim about seatbelts EXCEPT

A. statistics.

B. urgent appeals.

C. dire warnings.

D. historical data.

ANSWERS TO DRILLS

Drill #1: Main idea/purpose questions

1. The passage states that, "Many criminologists assert that television dramas are affecting the way that court cases are adjudicated," and answer choice (D) offers the best paraphrase. The passage does not assert that forensic science needs to speed up, but that jurors' expectations need to be "slowed down" and "grounded in reality." So answer choice (A) is out. Answer choice (B) is too general, and answer choice (C) is never mentioned.

2. Answer choice (A) states the main idea very succinctly; the ACT is "enjoying a new wave of popularity." The passage does state that the SAT has "come under some criticism," but this isn't the main idea, nor does the author offer an opinion. Eliminate answer choices (B) and (C). Answer choice (D) is also incorrect, because "the best measure of [a student's] chances to succeed in college" is never mentioned.

3.   Answer choice (B) refers to a "similarity"—that "plant hormones exist in a similarly tiered system" to mammal hormones, and this is the main idea of the passage. Answer choice (A) is mentioned but never answered. Answer choice (C) is too general, and since no opinion is offered, there's no reason to select answer choice (D).

Drill #2: Specific reference questions

1.   Answer choice (C) is the best, because the passage says "the company that establishes the most effective means of mass production and distribution." You can eliminate answer choice (A) right away, because the "traditional" way doesn't work anymore. Answer choices (B) and (C) are never mentioned.

2.   The passage states that Kepler was "one of the first medieval scientists to analyze a phenomenon rather than argue over theories. . . ." Answer choice (A) is the best because it is uses dispute as a paraphrase of "argue over theories." Answer choice (C) describes what Kepler did rather than others. Answer choices (B) and (D) are never mentioned.

3.   The passage refers to "literary dualism" that "stemmed from her own difficulties to reconcile contradictory perceptions of herself." The best answer is choice (C). That the perceptions can be deceiving (A) was not indicated. Answer choices (B) and (D) are never mentioned.

Drill #3: Inference questions

1.   The entirety of the passage discusses how genetics affects "the frequency with which bipolar disorder is genetically inherited" and backs it up with statistics. Therefore, it must be true that "a person's risk of developing bipolarism is at least partially determined by genetic factors." The best answer is choice (A). We don't know about grandparents, so answer choice (B) can be eliminated. We also know nothing about siblings, or whether the diagnoses are increasing. So answer choices (C) and (D) are incorrect.

2. We know that answer choice (D) is correct, because $3 worth of grass and $7 worth of barley totals $10 per year, and $1 per month of wheat translates to $12 per year. Therefore, the best answer is (D). Answer choice (A) might be tempting, but we don't know anything about quantity (just monetary value). Answer choices (B) and (C) can't be defended by what is in the passage.

3. In the last sentence, the passage first refers to T cells, which inflict damage on the protective coatings. Since the passage mentions that "the body's immune system" was thought to be attacking these coatings, so it must be true that T cells are part of the immune system. The best answer is (B). Answer choices (A), (C) and (D) cannot be defended by what is in the passage.

ANSWERS TO SAMPLE QUESTIONS

1. The passage talks about two perceptions of Florence Nightingale, one negative and one positive. The best answer is (D). Answer choice (A) discusses only one side of the debate, and neither answer choice (B) nor (C) mentions Nightingale, making them too general.

2. The passage implies that, if the stock price dropped, a huge sale "would give larger investors a considerable advantage over smaller ones." Those who owned 20 percent or more of a company would unfairly earn a short-term profit. The best answer is (B). Answer choices (A), (C) and (D) are not mentioned.

3. The passage is about the Organic Act of 1900 and its "immediate and powerful impact on Hawaiian commerce." Therefore, the best answer choice is (D). There is no opinion offered about whether plantations were flawed, so answer choice (A) is out. Answer choice (B) is way too broad, since it talks about all Pacific islanders. And the "plight of illegally imported contract laborers" is never mentioned.

4.   Like many reading comprehension passages, this paragraph involves a new study that challenges a widely held opinion. This passage discusses perceptions of meteor streams tracked by new computer software that experienced "two periods of peak density," which were associated with a stream that is "hollow at its center." Therefore, it must be true that a stream without a hollow center would have "one specific peak." The best answer is (D).

5.   Critics are not mentioned in the passage until the last sentence, where it is stated that "the critic can use his or her body of knowledge to facilitate the exchange of ideas." Answer choice (B) paraphrases this idea adeptly.

6.   The passage shares details of the two separate criteria of the two scales. The Richter scale is based on "the energy that the earthquake releases," and the modified Mercalli measures the "earthquake's effect on the people and/or buildings above." The best answer choice is (A). There is no mention of whether one scale is more accurate than the other, or that they are used together, so answer choices (B) and (C) can be struck. Answer choice (D) might seem like an easy assumption, but the passage doesn't say either way. And when you think of it, a very strong earthquake that takes place in a barren area would score high on the Richter scale but low on the Mercalli.

7.   The passage states that gelatin created a less distorted image than "ever before." Therefore, we can infer that gelatin produced more authentic images than collodion. None of the other answer choices is defensible using the text of the passage, so the best answer choice is (D).

8.   The passage discusses how and why people (and by extension, society) create heroes. The best answer choice is (B). Heroism is never identified as "inconsistent" or "unnecessary," so you can get rid of answer choices (A) and (C). And regardless of whether you agree with the attractive sentiment in answer choice (D), there is no mention of it in the passage.

9.   The passage mentions that "many private schools delay reading instruction in favor of basic classes in phonetics and storytelling." Therefore, these schools believe that reading instruction in kindergarten is "premature," and the best answer choice is (C).

10. The passage uses statistics saying that "in 1930, an estimated 30,000 people died every year from vehicular accidents," historical data that showed that "doctors urged car manufacturers to make the seatbelt standard on all vehicles, as they were on aircraft," and warnings saying that, "without a seatbelt, a body's forward momentum would send it forward violently, often resulting in serious bodily injury." Although the author clearly lauds the use of seatbelts, there is no mention of specific appeals to use them. The best answer choice is (B).

CHAPTER 4: *Relating Sentences*

"It's a mini-exercise in reading comprehension, with only two types of questions and a handful of possible answers."

- Part IV of the Accuplacer's verbal portion consists of 10 questions in which you are presented with two sentences and asked to determine how the sentences are related. It's a skill associated with reading comprehension, and the Accuplacer's preparation materials treat it like that. Since these questions have their own separate section on the test, however, we've given them their own chapter. Although the analytic skills you will need on Parts III and IV of the Accuplacer are similar, the Relating Sentences questions are very different from the questions in Part III for two reasons:

- There's a lot less reading involved.

- The answer choices fall into only a few very specific categories.

What they look like

Each Relating Sentences question starts with two sentences:

New York's Taxi and Limousine Commission requires that proprietors of taxi-cabs in New York City be proficient in the English language.

Nearly half of the residents of New York City speak a language other than English when at home with their families.

The question then asks one of two questions about those sentences:

- What does the second sentence do?

- How are the two sentences related?

And in keeping with the rest of the test, there are four answer choices:

A   It restates the claim made in the first sentence.

B   It sums up the points raised in the first sentence.

C   It provides an example for what is stated in the first sentence.

D   It gives unexpected information.

Process of elimination

If you thought that Reading Comprehension questions were especially susceptible to the Process of Elimination, wait until you try these. Later in this chapter, we'll discuss the few types of answer choices that appear repeatedly on these questions. For now, let's take a look at that first question and show how so much of this process relies merely on common sense.

How to answer them

Let's look at the question again, in its entirety:

New York's Taxi and Limousine Commission requires that proprietors of taxi-cabs in New York City be proficient in the English language.

Nearly half of residents of New York City speak a language other than English when at home with their families.

What does the second sentence do?

      A It restates the claim made in first sentence.

      B It sums up the points raised in the first sentence.

      C It provides an example for what is stated in the first sentence.

      D It gives unexpected information.

The first sentence asserts that taxi drivers have to possess some level of fluency in English in order to be sanctioned to drive. The second, however, says that English is the primary language of nearly half of the city's households. Therefore, it implies that the Taxi and Limousine Commission's rule might not be all that necessary, or even relevant. If you had to choose whether the two sentences express similar or divergent ideas, you would pick the latter.

Now let's look at the answer choices and get ready to cross things off. Answer choice (A) is immediately expendable, because the second sentence doesn't restate anything from the first. For similar reasons, you can cross off answer choices (B) and (C), which also rely on the sentences having a mutually supportive role. That leaves only answer choice (D), which fits nicely with the second sentence's contradictory tone.

And here's an important point: You might not necessarily agree that the information in the second sentence was "unexpected." What you must agree with, however, is that answer choice (D) is definitely the best of the four answers you were given. All of this underscores the point we've made from the beginning: It's not important what's perfect, only what's *best*.

COMMON RELATIONSHIPS

Once you get a look at a number of these questions, you'll notice that the answer choices tend to repeat themselves again and again. In fact, you can sort most of them into one of the following categories:

1. The sentences provide support for (or repeat) each other

In much the same way as we solved the sample problem above, it's often a good first strategy to decide if the sentences are on the same side, or opposite sides of "the fence." Once you make that decision, you can usually eliminate at least two of your answer choices. If you're asked how the two sentences relate to each other, they might support each other, like this:

> *Cars that can achieve the most miles per gallon can save an average house-hold hundreds of dollars per year.*

> *Greater fuel efficiency lowers wear-and-tear on a car's engine, which prolongs its life and decreases the cost and frequency of repairs.*

In this case, both statements center on how it's better to have a fuel-efficient car instead of a gas guzzler.

2. The sentences contradict (or provide contrast to) each other.

If the statements don't agree with each other, then it's possible that one may state the opposite of the other:

> *In the current labor dispute, team owners assert that the sour economy has reduced their revenues.*

> *Studies show that, in hard financial times, sports fans tend to distract them-selves by attending more live sporting events.*

In this case, the first sentence says the owners have less money, but the second suggests that the opposite is true. So they contradict each other. Note: This relationship can also be stated in a similar way as our first example, where the second sentence provided "unexpected" information.

3. The second sentence indicates a problem or gives a solution.

Another common relationship is for one sentence to indicate a problem, and the other suggests a solution to that problem. The sentences usually appear in that order, but it's not unprecedented for them to appear in reverse:

> *Faced with an inability to sell them, boat owners have been scuttling their watercraft offshore in order to avoid the maintenance expense.*

> *Governments of coastal states have offered to buy unwanted boats and use them to create artificial reefs that benefit specific fish populations.*

Sentence 1 states the problem that boat owners are sinking their boats wherever they want to, and Sentence 2 provides a way to solve the problem by suggesting that the boats could be bought and used in ways that could actually benefit the ecosystem.

4. The second sentence states a cause or effect.

It's possible for the two sentences to have a cause-and-effect relationship, like this:

> *The turn of the 21st century saw a boom in the number of investors who bought stock in individual companies rather than in mutual funds.*

> *Technology, education, and competition have allowed investors to buy a company's shares without the expensive fees a traditional broker charges.*

The first sentence describes the new trend of investing directly in companies, and the second suggests three reasons why that trend has taken place.

5. The second sentence gives an example.

This relationship is very similar to the first one in this list. The main difference is that the first sentence describes a general situation, and the second supports that with a specific piece of evidence, like this:

> *The current political climate has resulted in an overall effort to increase liberties rather than curb them.*

> *In the past two years, seven states have watered down laws against carrying a concealed weapon in a government building.*

The second sentence is indeed supportive, but there is a specific framework of one sentence being an abstract assertion, and the second providing concrete evidence of that assertion. If you're concerned about this distinction, don't be. The test writers need one answer choice to be clearly better than the other three, so you're very unlikely to have to choose between a choice that reads, "The second sentence provides support" and, "The second sentence provides an example." These answers are too similar in tone, and writers of the Accuplacer (or any test, for that matter) don't want to create an opportunity for a dispute.

6. The second sentence draws a conclusion.

This relationship is pretty straightforward; the first sentence provides information, and the second concludes something based on that information:

> *Increased use of pesticides in sub-Saharan Africa has greatly reduced mosquito populations.*

> *Humanitarian groups in Africa will likely see a profound drop in the number of cases of mosquito-borne malaria among the humans they treat.*

In this example, if there are fewer mosquitoes attacking humans, it stands to reason that there will be less malaria to treat.

7. It provides an application for a theory.

This is another very specific relationship, whereby the first sentence provides a theory, and the second offers a possible way to test it or put it to good use:

> *Young adults who rely less on outside support tend to develop a very strong work ethic.*

> *A college student paying his way through college will show greater commitment to schoolwork than one whose parents are footing the tuition bill.*

The second sentence deals only with one student, not all "young adults." So the second sentence applies the rule mentioned in the first sentence to one specific situation. This is somewhat like providing "an example" (again, you're not likely to see both "application" and "example" in the same set of answer choices), but it's different from "restating" the same idea as the first sentence.

8. The second sentence provides an analysis (or an explanation).

In this last example, the first sentence might provide information that seems unexpected or paradoxical, and the second offers a way to reconcile the first:

> *Despite a recent rise in incidents of urban crime, families are moving to cities in record rates.*

> *Social media and other methods of networking help families find the safest neighborhoods in which to live.*

In the first sentence, it might seem odd for families to move to cities when urban crime is on the rise, but the second sentence exposes the common misconception that crime rates are universal among all neighborhoods. Instead, it suggests that some neighborhoods are safer than others, and that the families have several tools at their disposal in order to move to the city and avoid the more crime-ridden areas.

SAMPLE QUESTIONS

Try these sample Relating Sentences questions. The answers are on page 101.

1. *Owning and maintaining a car can be tremendously expensive.*

   Many people who live in cities say they do so partly because they don't need to own a car.

   What does the second sentence do?

   A. It states an effect.

   B. It gives an example.

   C. It lends support.

   D. It offers a contrary opinion.

2. *The average fast-food hamburger has double the calories and sodium than it did five years ago.*

   Many fast-food restaurants are offering more healthful menu options such as fruit and salads.

   How are the sentences related?

   A. They contradict each other.

   B. They present a solution to a problem.

   C. They repeat the same information.

   D. They support a general rule using specific examples.

3. *For the past several weeks, teachers have been gathering to protest widespread cuts in the education budget.*

   In defending the decision, the governor cited a sharp drop in tax revenue.

   What does the second sentence do?

   A. It reconciles contrary opinions.

   B. It provides an explanation for an unpopular action.

   C. It exemplifies the first sentence.

   D. It suggests a solution.

4. *The ice storm has left all streets and sidewalks precariously slippery.*

   Due to safety reasons, all schools and government buildings are closed.

   What does the second sentence do?

   A. It states the cause.

   B. It makes a comparison.

   C. It gives an example.

   D. It states the effect.

5. *Music education helps elementary school students develop logical thinking and study skills.*

   My brother's grades have improved greatly since he took up the clarinet.

   How are the two sentences related?

   A. One uses a specific example to support a general point asserted in the other.

   B. They contradict each other.

   C. One states a potential solution to a problem stated in the other.

   D. They state the same information.

6. *Studies show that many video games can bring about epilepsy in young children.*

   Sales of video-game systems have tripled over the past decade.

   What does the second sentence do?

   A. It laments an alarming trend.

   B. It gives unexpected information.

   C. It draws a conclusion.

   D. It states an example.

7. *The North Atlantic silver perch has been put on the list of endangered species list.*

Commercial fishermen have been overfishing Scandinavian waters without proper attention to re-stocking.

What does the second sentence do?

A. It provides an application for a theory.

B. It provides a contrast.

C. It debunks a dubious assumption.

D. It states a possible cause.

8. *Economists show that consumers have less discretionary income to spend on luxury items.*

The record cold this winter has increased the average homeowner's heating bill by 16%.

How are the two sentences related?

A. They offer contrasting views of a contentious debate.

B. They relate consistent information.

C. They provide a general rule and a specific example.

D. They show evidence of a popular misconception.

9. *Professional golfers are known for their ability to maintain an even emotional keel despite any external circumstances.*

   Taking standardized tests is like playing golf, because both depend on how well you recover from mistakes.

   What does the second sentence do?

   A. It states the effect of a cause.

   B. It offers a solution.

   C. It makes a comparison.

   D. It extols a specific skill.

10. *Now more than ever, professional athletes must adhere to an off-season regimen in order to maintain their peak physical condition.*

    Athletes who are out of shape when they arrive in training camp are in danger of losing their jobs to those who can outperform them physically.

    What does the second sentence do?

    A. It restates the claim made in the first sentence.

    B. It exemplifies a trend asserted in the first sentence.

    C. It sums up the points made in the first sentence.

    D. It attempts to contradict the first sentence using irrelevant information.

ANSWERS TO SAMPLE QUESTIONS

1. The first sentence asserts that it costs a lot of money to own a car, so it follows logically that people would decide to live in the city in order to avoid the expense of a car. The second sentence, therefore, lends support to the first. The best answer is (C).

2. The second sentence states that fast-food restaurants are offering more healthful menu items, but information in the first sentence suggests the opposite, because the hamburgers have more calories and sodium. Therefore, the sentences contradict each other, and the best answer is (A).

3. The first sentence refers to a decision that has been deemed unpopular, because people are protesting it. In the second, the governor attempts to defend, or explain, the decision by citing a sharp drop in tax revenue. This explanation makes (B) the best choice.

4. These two sentences have a basic cause-and-effect relationship. The cause is the ice storm, and the effect is that all schools and government buildings have been closed. The second sentence, therefore, is the effect of the cause presented in the first sentence. The best answer is (D).

5. The first sentence is a general statement linking music education and logical thinking and study skills. The second sentence introduces a specific example that strengthens this link. The best answer is (A).

6. Based on the potentially alarming information stated in the first sentence, one might expect people to avoid video-game systems. The second sentence, however, states the reverse, that sales of video-game systems are improving. This information is "unexpected," so the best answer is (B).

7. The first sentence asserts that the North Atlantic silver perch is endangered, and the second suggests that Scandinavian waters (which are in the North Atlantic) have been overfished. This is a potential cause for the first sentence. The best answer is (D).

8. The first sentence says people have less money to spend on luxury items, and the idea that people are spending more to heat their homes is consistent information. The best answer is (B).

9. The first sentence asserts that professional golfers achieve a certain skill that helps them excel in competition. The second refers to golfers in an entirely different way by comparing them to those who take standardized tests, because they require a similar skill set. The best answer is (C).

10. These two sentences are solid paraphrases of each other, and each asserts that in order for professional athletes to succeed, they must stay in peak physical condition all year round. The best answer is (A).

CHAPTER 5: *Essay Writing*

"Tell them what you're going to say, tell them what you have to say, and then tell them what you just said."

The last task of your Accuplacer experience will be to write an essay on a topic that will be provided for you. Of all five parts of the Accuplacer, the essay has the most fluid guidelines. You might have to take it, or you might not. You might have to type it, or you'll have to submit it on paper. It might be timed, or it might be open-ended. All of these decisions will be made by the individual school that administers the test.

For the purposes of this chapter, then, we're going assume the strictest parameters possible and treat the essay as if (1) you have to take it, and (2) you have a time limit. Whether you have to type or write it isn't that big a deal, unless you have terrible typing skills or undecipherable handwriting. There are things to keep in mind for each format, however, and we'll address those as well.

The *How*, Not the *What*

A college or university might want to test your essay-writing skills because so much of your college experience will involve expressing your ideas in print as eloquently as possible. It's important to note that the essay readers will not judge you by *what you say*—i.e., what your thesis statement is. They will be much more interested in *how you say it*. So if you take the controversial position that the minimum age of a member of Congress should be lowered from 25 to 13, for example, you can get a good score if you write well and defend your assertion shrewdly, whether or not the reader agrees with you.

THE FIVE POINTS

The most concrete advice that the Accuplacer has to offer in terms of how to write its essay is a checklist of the five elements that the Accuplacer's essay readers will look for in your writing. These are the core ideas that every essay writer should learn and, for the purposes of this test, practice over and over. After you gain some more experience with these essays, you might be surprised to find that the skills will come more naturally to you, without your having to think about them.

Element 1: Mechanics

The first thing essay readers will notice about your essay is whether your sentences are grammatically sound. These readers have been around the block a few thousand times when it comes to reading essays, so errors in grammar, spelling, or syntax will tend to really stand out. And in most readers' minds, nothing compromises the value of an essay more than a poor understanding of the basic rules of written English.

Luckily, if you've had the chance to study grammar rather intensely for the first two sections of the Accuplacer, you may have already noticed that your grammar skills have improved. When you finish any essay, you should always re-read it to look for mistakes you may have made in your first draft. Even if your essay is timed, you should always leave a little time at the end to refine and polish your work.

Element 2: Structure

The structure of an essay involves the variety of sentences that you use. There are many ways to construct a sentence, and each has its own rhythm. If you repeat the same sentence structure throughout a paragraph, the reader will get really bored really fast. Consider this:

> *France is a big country. It is in the middle of Europe. Its capital is Paris. Paris has a population of 2.2 million people. The city is known for its beautiful buildings. One of these buildings is the Cathedral of Notre Dame.*

Are you asleep yet? The rhythm of the sentences is so repetitive that it lulls you into expecting what's next, and it makes the reader feel he just drank a bottle of cough syrup. Now, consider the same information expressed in this way:

> *Located at the center of Europe, France has the second-largest land mass on the continent. Paris, its capital city, has a population of 2.2 million people, and its architecture—including the world-famous Cathedral of Notre Dame—stands out for its beauty and historical significance.*

See the difference? After a little more added information, the sentences are varied, they contain a wider array of vocabulary, and they flow into each other better. The result: A much higher score.

Element 3: Organization

When you were younger, you may have learned the most basic way to organize an essay: An introductory paragraph that contains a thesis statement, two or three paragraphs that support the statement made in the introduction, and a strong concluding paragraph. One way to look at this three-part scheme is with these three statements:

- Tell them what you're going to say;

- Say what you have to say; and

- Tell them what you just said.

It might seem over-simple, but simplicity is the name of the game when you're writing an essay on a standardized test. The readers have a lot of essays to read, and they don't have a lot of time to linger on your magnum opus.

Element 4: Development

Readers like organization, and they like when your ideas are developed well in the body of your essay. Are your examples interesting? Are they relevant to your thesis? Are they linked together well?

Element 5: Focus

This speaks to the overall feel of your essay, which your reader will appreciate once he or she has read the entire thing. Is your message clear, or did you derail your train of thought? Do your paragraphs progress logically? Essentially, the reader wants to assess how well you understood the topic and how well your body paragraphs supported your thesis statement. Again, it's important to remember that the reader doesn't care as much about the thesis statement itself as about how well that statement is supported, and that the overall message is compelling.

The (Unofficial) Sixth Point

When you write your essay, try to put yourself in your reader's position. Your reader will be reading a lot of these essays at once, and some of them will be . . . not as good at the others. A number will have bad handwriting, bad spelling, no paragraphs, no clear focus, muddled or nonexistent reasoning, etc. Reading so many essays is already a difficult task, and essays with problems like these make the reader's work all the more arduous. Making a reader work hard is always a bad thing.

Conversely, if your reader surfaces from several challenging essays in a row to find your well-organized work, containing relevant examples to support a clear thesis statement, he or she will be overjoyed.

THE APPROACH

When faced with an essay question, your first instinct might be to get right to it and start writing (or typing). But remember: You're being assessed on how focused and organized you are, so it's never a good idea to start rambling and hope that whatever you end up with makes any sense. Instead, use the following four steps to create an essay that best measures up to the criteria we've outlined above. If you take the time to structure and think before you write, you may find that the writing flows a lot more easily.

Step 1: Brainstorm

After you read the essay prompt, take a few moments to think about how you might answer it. Do you have an opinion? If so, write it down. If not, start thinking about examples that would be relevant to the topic. Anything is possible: personal anecdotes, books you've read, movies you've seen, current events, etc. Write all of these down, too, and whatever you do, don't censor yourself. Free-think with as few restrictions as possible; you'll have plenty of time to sift through all the ideas as you prepare for step 2.

Notice that we haven't said anything about forming an opinion (or a thesis statement) yet, since at this point you don't really need to have one. In some cases, you might not formulate your thesis until after you've had a look at some of the ideas you've written down. As in many elements of this or any standardized test, don't discount the possibility of a mid-problem epiphany. They're much more common than you might think.

Step 2: Make An Outline

This is where your essay finds its structure and sounds less like your free-associative ramblings. Look among all the ideas you jotted down. Which ones seem the most relevant? Which seem to fit together to form the most effective thesis? Keep the ones you like, skip the ones you don't, and get ready to build the skeleton of your essay.

Step 3: Start Writing Informally

Most of us think in conversational English, rather than formal, written English. So as you're forming your essay, indulge your instincts and start writing as if you're explaining your ideas to a friend. Expressing your thoughts informally can actually speed the creative process, because you won't feel compelled to express them in the most formal way possible. This also makes your ideas come across as more genuine.

Step 4: Polish It Up

Once you feel your essay's content is strong, and your ideas are fully formed and supported well, it's time to formalize your writing into something that might appear in published form. Use this time to:

- read the essay start to finish to see if your paragraphs flow well together ("connecting" words like *Furthermore* can be useful);

- make sure your paragraphs are reasonably short (4-8 sentences) and strongly delineated;

- rewrite sentences to make sure they don't all have the same rhythm;

- insert synonyms to vary your word choice;

- check for spelling, syntax, and punctuation.

As you finish up your work, it's important to note here that even though your ability to write a thoughtful, concise essay is being tested, your readers also know this is an impromptu exercise with, in many cases, a deadline. They are looking for an essay of high quality, but they also know they cannot expect perfection on such an off-the-cuff assignment. This realization may take a little pressure off you as you endeavor to create your best work under pressure. All you can do is the best you can do, and practice will help you improve.

WORKING STEP BY STEP

Let's put the steps we just discussed into practice and write an essay. Here's a sample prompt:

"Courtesy is disappearing from everyday interactions, and as a result, we are all the poorer for it."

To what extent do you agree with this statement? Explain your position by writing a unified essay using relevant reasons and/or examples from your own experience, observations, or reading.

OK. We have our topic, and it's a great one. As you contemplate an answer, you can go in any of several directions. Try a little brainstorming for ideas relevant to this topic. How many overlap with these?

- people text and e-mail instead of talk

- people don't even phone anymore (article I read in the paper)

- Internet makes for lots of superficial friendships instead of a few meaningful ones

- TV show I saw about faces and how they can help disputes

- cars—road rage because can't see faces

- too much pressure to work and achieve; not enough time to sit back and be pleasant with people

- people in every generation think the next one thinks less about manners than their own

- positives of social media and networking: Texting to help Red Cross in Haiti and Japan. Spreads information more quickly and can mobilize more people to help in various ways.

Now, formulate your thesis and make an outline:

Paragraph 1: People think courtesy is disappearing, but I don't think it's true. Three reasons why.

Paragraph 2: Acknowledge why people feel this way. Studies: people interact better when they can see people's faces. Road rage is prevalent, mostly because you can't see faces. Social media and the Internet change the way we relate. Not as much face time.

Paragraph 3: Our corporate culture is pressuring people to achieve, at all costs. People often list common courtesy as one of the most common casualties.

Paragraph 4: Common refrain, however. As people age, they focus more on quality of life, less so with younger people. Makes sense that older people would take younger people to task.

Paragraph 5: Good things the Internet has done. Kiva.org. Texting $$ to Red Cross. Facebook. Easier to keep current.

Paragraph 6: Conclusion. People commonly assume that common courtesy is dying out. Society changes, new challenges arise. But people are still ultimately out to help each other out in times of crisis.

First Draft

Now that you have an outline, you can start writing your essay with a firm idea of what topic(s) each paragraph will cover. You might be surprised how quickly the words come when you put together your first draft:

> *People think courtesy is disappearing, because social networking is taking the place of face-to-face networking. E-mail is replacing the handshake. While that may be true in a small sense, I believe that man's desire to help out his fellow man remains strong, and that social networking is actually helping to facilitate that goodwill.*
>
> *It's true that "everyday interactions" are changing. As evidenced by the popularity of Facebook, Twitter, and other social networking platforms, more people are interacting artificially, without face-to-face contact. The advancement of smart phones makes it easier for people to text rather than talk to each other. And studies about road rage, for example, show that people interact better when they can see each other's faces.*
>
> *Despite these concerns, however, I believe that complaining about common courtesy is a common refrain from one generation to the next. Younger people tend to be more ambitious and driven toward more discovering themselves. As people age, however, they can focus*

less on their financial station and more on the quality of the society they live in. If they perceive that society has changed since "their day," it is common for older people to take younger people to task.

In addition, I believe not enough attention is paid to all the benefits that social networking has brought us. Facebook has helped reform-ers bring about regime change in several Middle Eastern countries, such as Egypt and Yemen. Kiva.org helps people loan small amounts of money to others for whom a small donation can make a world of difference. Texting has made it easy to donate money to the Red Cross as it comes to the aid of earthquake victims in Haiti and Japan.

People commonly assume that common courtesy is dying out, and social media is the common culprit. The truth, however, is that societ-ies change, and the ever-changing technological landscape is always posing new challenges to what some perceive as common courtesy. But even if that were true, the level of grass-roots philanthropy that has helped hundreds of thousands in crisis makes a nice trade-off.

Once your first draft is complete, take a look at it. Does it flow well? Do all the elements fit?

You may have noticed that Paragraph 3 in the outline was omitted from the first draft. It might have looked good in the outline stage, but the author's thesis is to disagree with the given statement. Therefore, it doesn't make sense to include another para-graph that acknowledged the opposite viewpoint. And secondly, as the essay took shape, it adhered more to the theme of social networking. So whatever you thought in terms of the assertion made in the Old Paragraph 3, it was ultimately deemed off-topic.

Don't discount the potential for a mid-essay epiphany when you write your response. As you write, you will be sifting ideas in your mind all the time. Changes in your way of thinking are quite likely, and it's easy to accommodate them.

Review and refine

Now let's take a look at where we can refine the language a bit and add a little polish. The changes we've made are in **bold**:

Some people **believe** that courtesy is disappearing, because social networking is taking the place of face-to-face networking. The **antiseptic** e-mail is replacing the **warm** handshake. While that may be true in a small sense, I believe that man's desire to help out his fellow man remains strong, and that social networking is actually helping to facilitate that goodwill.

It is **easy to make the case** that "everyday interactions" are changing. As evidenced by the popularity of Facebook, Twitter, and other social networking platforms, more people are interacting **artificially**, without personal contact. The advancement of smart phones makes it easier for people to text rather than talk to each other. And as studies about road rage ha**ve shown**, for example, people **are more aggressive toward each other when they interact without the cordiality of face-to-face exchange.**

Despite these concerns, however, I believe that **bemoaning the demise of** courtesy is a common refrain from one generation to the next. Younger people tend to be more ambitious and driven toward more discovering **who they are and what they want.** As people age, however, they can focus less on their financial station and more on the quality of the society they live in. If they perceive that society has changed since "their day," it is common for older people to take younger people to task.

In addition, I believe not enough attention is paid to all the benefits that social networking has brought us. Facebook has helped reformers bring about regime change in several Middle Eastern countries, such as Egypt and Yemen. Kiva.org helps people loan small amounts of money to others for whom a small donation can make a world of *difference. Texting has made it easy to donate money to the Red Cross as it comes to earthquake victims in Haiti and Japan.*

People commonly assume that common courtesy is dying out, and social media is **often demonized as the culprit***. The truth, however, is that societies change, and the ever-changing technological landscape is always posing new challenges to what some perceive as common courtesy. But even if that were true, the level of grass-roots philanthropy that has helped hundreds of thousands in crisis* **more than makes up for it.**

And now you have your final product, ready for review. It's only 369 words, but it's concise, structured well, and discusses the issue using relevant information. It also features varied sentence structure and word choice.

OTHER STYLE POINTS

When you're working through your final read-through, keep these other ideas in mind:

- **Acknowledge the other side:** Your stance on a particular subject becomes much more compelling if you can display an understanding of why those who disagree with you feel the way they do. This shows that you've considered both sides of the debate and cultivated an informed opinion.

- **Make sure it's long enough:** Readers can't help it. If an essay looks short, it will look incomplete, regardless of how well you turn a phrase within. (Would you have bought this book if it were only 50 pages long?) Take the time to brainstorm as thoroughly as you can about the essay prompt and bring as much detail into your discussion as possible.

- **Don't repeat yourself:** If you come up with what you think is a really trenchant idea, your instinct might be to repeat that idea more than once in order to make sure the reader saw your fantastic insight. When you repeat thoughts, it shows that you're basing your thesis on fewer ideas than it might look like, and essay readers can see through that ploy from several miles away.

- **Be resolute:** Your job as a writer is to compel your reader to share your thoughts. If you're wishy-washy about what you're trying to say, how can you expect your reader to be persuaded? Instead of saying this *may be* a problem, say it *is* a problem. The more convinced you are, the more convinced they will be.

- If you're writing your essay, try to write as legibly as possible. Deciphering sloppy work is about as hard a job as a reader has.

- If you're typing your essay, brush up on your typing skills. If you spend all your time hunting and pecking, you'll take time away from your planning and composition, and your essay will suffer.

SAMPLE ESSAY TOPICS

As always, better writing comes from practice. Try writing an essay using each of these essay prompts. Once you're done, compare your work with the sample answers we've included at the end of this chapter.

ESSAY PROMPTS

For each of the following essay prompts, write a unified essay indicating the extent to which you agree with the statement. Use relevant reasons and/or examples from your own experience, observations, or reading.

1. "Schools should be as responsible for teaching ethical and social values as they are for academic skills."

2. "The study of history runs counter to our best interests, because it prevents us from focusing on the challenges of the present."

3. "Self-interest and fear are the two most common forces that motivate people."

SAMPLE ESSAY ANSWERS

"Schools should be as responsible for teaching ethical and social values as they are for academic skills."

The premise of this statement is fundamentally flawed. First, ethical values and academics skills are not worthy of comparison because the two are so very different. Academic skills can be debated, but ethics are often debated far more passionately—especially when it comes to religion. And lastly, I believe that any parent who lets his or her child learn about ethics from a teacher is abdicating his responsibility.

First of all, social values cannot be treated or discussed in the same way as academic skills. Since most educators and parents have a good idea about the skills each student should have upon leaving high school, academic skills are easier to standardize. Ethical values, however, are far more subjective and vary more widely from home to home.

Secondly, ethical and social values are often tied to a person's religious beliefs, which are famously varied among people in the United States. Teaching a homogenized sense of good and evil could be perceived as siding with one religion over another. People are also much more passionate about core beliefs, religious or otherwise, than they are about academics. For example, a parent is unlikely to dispute whether his daughter should know what the Pythagorean Theorem is. However, he might react much more strongly about a religious rite, such as covering your body in public, and resent if a teacher told his daughter it was okay not to wear a burka.

Apart from the various religious customs that sometimes separate us, it is comforting to believe that all people share a common perception of what is right and wrong. I think that is true, but I also think that the job of imparting values to children lies with the parents, not with teachers. Teachers should be entrusted with helping a student learn what to know, but ultimately it is the parents who should help a child learn what to think.

"The study of history runs counter to our best interests, because it prevents us from focusing on the challenges of the present."

The author of this statement has presented an argument that is remarkably short-sighted. From the way he has phrased it, he appears to believe that the past and present are unrelated. This could not be further from the truth, as so much of what we decide in the present is informed by what we have already learned. Conversely, some of the hugest mistakes in American history have been made by those who, for whatever reason, ignored the lessons of the past.

The study of any science is a perfect example of how the past informs the present, as scientists are constantly using experimentation to build on what we already know. Seismologists, for example, studied the 1989 earthquake in San Francisco to see why some structural designs suffered terrible damage, while others escaped mostly unscathed. Architectural codes were revised to reflect this information, and the hope is that all new buildings, erected with state-of-the-art, earthquake-resistant foundations, will survive the subsequent seismic events that are guaranteed to come from the San Andreas Fault.

Our current economic climate serves as an excellent example of how important it is not to forget the past. After the Great Depression, Congress and President Franklin Roosevelt enacted several regulatory laws to protect against another steep drop in the stock market. One of these was the Glass-Steagall Act, which was designed to control speculation by separating investment banks from commercial banks. In the late 1990s, however, several powerful investment bankers successfully lobbied to have this Act repealed. With this regulation no longer in place, bankers saw fewer restrictions on their desire for greater profits. Among the results was the climate of predatory lending that bankrupted thousands of subprime mortgage holders, as well as the financial institutions that made these loans.

Most students of history will tell you that their studies have shown our existence to be cyclical. The best we can do when we experience disasters and other cataclysmic events is to learn from them and do our best to safeguard them from happening again. As George Santayana famously said, "Those who are unable to remember the past are condemned to repeat it."

"Self-interest and fear are the two most common forces that motivate people."

As jaded as this statement sounds, I believe there is more than a grain of truth to it.

First of all, I do not want to say that people are unwilling to help each other out. Most people I know are genuinely good people who are quick to lend a hand to a friend who needs it. And I've seen plenty of examples of pure altruism, where someone helps someone else without any expectations beyond a simple "Thank you." It is not uncommon, however, for a philanthropist to make a donation with a specific agenda. The billionaire who funds a new library might want his name across the top in order to create a certain image as a benefactor that could give him an advantage in business negotiations.

As a high school student, I know that a lot of the work I do stems from a desire to learn. But I also admit that I meet deadlines and take on unsavory tasks because I don't want to get in trouble with my parents or teachers. Without the threat of punishment, it would be easy for me to lapse into complacency and spend my time purely on things I wanted to do.

If you talked to my father about this topic, he would definitely steer the conversation to the stock market. After many years as a broker, he believes that the primary reasons why a market's level rises or falls are greed (the desire to buy into a stock that appears on the rise) and fear (the desire to sell out of a market that appears in free-fall). The ironic thing about stock volatility is that everyone is looking at what everyone else is doing, and this crowd mentality tends to make everyone feel the same thing at once, causing violent lurches in stock prices.

In conclusion, I do believe that most people are, at heart, mostly concerned with going after what they want. And in my experience, nothing gets me or my friends to do something more than the fear of what will happen if I don't do it. Without either of those pressures in my life, it's hard to imagine what I would accomplish, if anything.

Now that you've finished the subject review, it's time to jump into the practice tests. However, if you need some further brush-up on grammar and usage, along with a convenient glossary of frequently used terms, spend some time with our appendix materials, starting on page 189. We believe you'll find this to be a handy reference well beyond the Accuplacer test itself.

Accuplacer

Practice Test 1

ANSWER SHEET—PRACTICE TEST 1

PART I

1. Ⓐ Ⓑ Ⓒ Ⓓ
2. Ⓐ Ⓑ Ⓒ Ⓓ
3. Ⓐ Ⓑ Ⓒ Ⓓ

4. Ⓐ Ⓑ Ⓒ Ⓓ
5. Ⓐ Ⓑ Ⓒ Ⓓ
6. Ⓐ Ⓑ Ⓒ Ⓓ

7. Ⓐ Ⓑ Ⓒ Ⓓ
8. Ⓐ Ⓑ Ⓒ Ⓓ

9. Ⓐ Ⓑ Ⓒ Ⓓ
10. Ⓐ Ⓑ Ⓒ Ⓓ

PART II

11. Ⓐ Ⓑ Ⓒ Ⓓ
12. Ⓐ Ⓑ Ⓒ Ⓓ
13. Ⓐ Ⓑ Ⓒ Ⓓ
14. Ⓐ Ⓑ Ⓒ Ⓓ
15. Ⓐ Ⓑ Ⓒ Ⓓ
16. Ⓐ Ⓑ Ⓒ Ⓓ
17. Ⓐ Ⓑ Ⓒ Ⓓ
18. Ⓐ Ⓑ Ⓒ Ⓓ
19. Ⓐ Ⓑ Ⓒ Ⓓ
20. Ⓐ Ⓑ Ⓒ Ⓓ

_____
_____
_____
_____
_____
_____
_____
_____
_____
_____

PART III

21. Ⓐ Ⓑ Ⓒ Ⓓ
22. Ⓐ Ⓑ Ⓒ Ⓓ
23. Ⓐ Ⓑ Ⓒ Ⓓ

24. Ⓐ Ⓑ Ⓒ Ⓓ
25. Ⓐ Ⓑ Ⓒ Ⓓ
26. Ⓐ Ⓑ Ⓒ Ⓓ

27. Ⓐ Ⓑ Ⓒ Ⓓ
28. Ⓐ Ⓑ Ⓒ Ⓓ

29. Ⓐ Ⓑ Ⓒ Ⓓ
30. Ⓐ Ⓑ Ⓒ Ⓓ

PART IV

31. Ⓐ Ⓑ Ⓒ Ⓓ
32. Ⓐ Ⓑ Ⓒ Ⓓ
33. Ⓐ Ⓑ Ⓒ Ⓓ

34. Ⓐ Ⓑ Ⓒ Ⓓ
35. Ⓐ Ⓑ Ⓒ Ⓓ
36. Ⓐ Ⓑ Ⓒ Ⓓ

37. Ⓐ Ⓑ Ⓒ Ⓓ
38. Ⓐ Ⓑ Ⓒ Ⓓ

39. Ⓐ Ⓑ Ⓒ Ⓓ
40. Ⓐ Ⓑ Ⓒ Ⓓ

ANSWER SHEET

PART V

_____

_____

_____

_____

_____

_____

_____

_____

_____

_____

_____

_____

_____

_____

PART I

Select the best substitute for the underlined parts of the following ten sentences. The first answer [choice A] is identical to the original sentence. If you think the original sentence is best, then choose A as your answer.

1. Never before <u>such a technological marvel was witnessed by mankind</u>.

    A. such a technological marvel was witnessed by mankind

    B. has such a technological marvel been witnessed by mankind

    C. has mankind witnessed such a technological marvel

    D. by mankind had so technological a marvel been witnessed.

2. She used the money to repair her father's <u>boat, the one which he used</u> to sail from Maine to Florida.

    A. boat, the one which he used

    B. boat of which was used by him

    C. boat one which he used

    D. boat. The one which he used

3. While walking through the woods, <u>a soaring hawk was seen overhead by us</u>.

    A. a soaring hawk was seen overhead by us

    B. a hawk was seen by us soaring overhead

    C. a hawk's soaring overhead was seen by us

    D. we saw a hawk soaring overhead

4. <u>Who did your brother take</u> to the prom last year?

   A. Who did your brother take

   B. Whom did your brother take

   C. Who was taken by your brother

   D. Whom your brother took

5. Our museum owns a copy of The Mona <u>Lisa and the original is however</u> hanging in the Louvre in Paris.

   A. Lisa and the original is however

   B. Lisa but the original is however

   C. Lisa, the original, however, is hanging

   D. Lisa; the original, however, is hanging

6. He was suspended from the <u>team because he was late for</u> too many practices.

   A. team because he was late for

   B. team, as he was late for

   C. team, because of his lateness to

   D. team since his lateness to

7. Bill rented <u>the larger of the</u> four moving trucks.

   A. the larger of the

   B. the largest than

   C. the largest of the

   D. larger than the

8. I <u>wouldn't act so rashly if I was</u> you.

    A. wouldn't act to rashly if I was

    B. will act rashly if I am

    C. wouldn't act so rashly if I were

    D. wouldn't be acting rashly when I were

9. <u>Dennis, was perplexed by the tax forms, hired</u> an accountant.

    A. Dennis, was perplexed by the tax forms, hired

    B. Perplexed by the tax forms, Dennis hired

    C. Dennis was perplexed by the tax forms to hire

    D. Dennis was perplexed by the tax forms, hired

10. "May I take your <u>order?" said</u> the woman at the drive-through window.

    A. order?" said

    B. order"? said

    C. order," said

    D. order." said

PART II

Rewrite the following ten sentences mentally in your own head. Follow the directions given for the formation of the new sentence. Remember that your new sentence should be grammatically correct and convey the same meaning as the original sentence.

11.   Jonathan is a great saxophone player, and he is also a great trumpet player.

Rewrite, using: <u>not only</u>

Your new sentence will include:

A. but also a great trumpet player

B. as well as a great trumpet player

C. he also plays trumpet greatly

D. and also a great trumpet player

12.   She was delayed by traffic and arrived at the airport too late to make her flight.

Rewrite, beginning with: <u>Having been</u>

Your new sentence will include:

A. her arrival at the airport

B. she was arriving at the airport

C. she arrived at the airport

D. her flight left too early

13. The park ranger's warning about bears in the national park made me very nervous.

Rewrite, beginning with: <u>I was nervous when</u>

The next words will be:

A. the park ranger's warning

B. the park ranger warned

C. the park ranger, warning

D. the park ranger was warning

14. Unless he receives financing from his bank, he will not buy the car.

Rewrite, beginning with: <u>He will only</u>

The next words will be:

A. buy the car

B. not buy the car

C. receive financing

D. not receive financing

15. Flooded by the massive rainstorm, the road was blocked off from all car traffic.

Rewrite, beginning with: <u>The road</u>

Your new sentence will include:

A. because it was being

B. because it is

C. because of its being

D. because it was

16. The reporter was sent to prison because she refused to reveal her sources.

Rewrite, beginning with: <u>Because of</u>

The next words will be:

A. being sent to prison

B. the reporter's refusal

C. the reporter was refusing

D. the sources not being revealed

17. It's difficult for me to speak Italian, but I can speak Spanish very well.

Rewrite, beginning with: <u>Unlike Italian,</u>

The next words will be:

A. Spanish is easier

B. I can speak Spanish

C. speaking Spanish

D. I am speaking Spanish

18. In the event of a snowstorm, the city's sanitation department will work overtime.

Rewrite, beginning with: <u>If</u>

The next words will be:

A. it snows

B. snow is

C. snowing

D. snows

19. He is not able to go the beach because he has not finished his final exams.

Rewrite, beginning with: <u>If he had finished</u>

Your new sentence will include:

A. he will not be able

B. he would have been able

C. he is not able

D. he cannot

20. Despite many attempts, he was unable to ride the bull for more than five seconds.

Rewrite, beginning with: <u>Although</u>

The next words will be:

A. attempting

B. many attempts

C. he had been attempting

D. he attempted

PART III

For the following ten questions, read the passage and then select the correct answer to the question. You may need to answer based on explicit information from the passage, as well as ideas that are suggested or implied in the passage.

21. As immigrants left Ellis Island, some headed for New York, but others bought tickets to board the Central Railroad of New Jersey (CRRNJ) and traveled by train to their new homes. As the population of the United States increased throughout the 1800s, the need for railway transportation in and out of New Jersey became more obvious. In 1864, the CRRNJ built its first railroad terminal where people could purchase tickets and board trains. As immigration increased, a second terminal was constructed in 1889. This terminal, located near what is now the northern part of Liberty State Park, still stands today as an important part of American history.

    The main purpose of this passage is to

    A. provide a comprehensive history of the CRRNJ.

    B. discuss the increase of rail travel during the immigration boom.

    C. debunk the myth that all immigrants stayed in New York City.

    D. state that the increase in train travel could not keep pace with the rate of immigration.

22. In the spring of 2010, the explosive eruption of an Icelandic volcano disrupted airplane routes in and out of Europe for weeks. The enormous ash cloud that shrouded much of the North Atlantic Ocean was bad enough, but pilots were particularly concerned about sudden rises and drops in the height of the cloud, which made flying over it more unpredictable and dangerous. Researchers may have found a way to solve this problem by analyzing the ash cloud's static electricity, which is eventually discharged as bolts of lightning.

    We can conclude from the information in the passage that

    A. volcanoes generate static electricity.

B. if another ash cloud forms over the Atlantic, pilots will likely have less trouble flying over it.

C. pilots were more concerned about static electricity than the lack of visibility.

D. scientists could have foreseen when the Icelandic ash cloud was created.

23. Setting out a birdfeeder is a common practice in most residential areas. By some estimations, for example, feeders provide nourishment for as many as 30 million birds in Great Britain per year. Despite this fact, however, a scientist in Switzerland has concluded that feeding birds might not be in their best interest. Some male birds, after going without food all night, need to arise early and sing a dawn chorus in order to attract a female. In general, males that sing earliest attract the best mates. When food was introduced overnight, however, 36% of the males didn't start singing until after sunrise, indicating that the well-fed birds became lazy and more ill-prepared to mate and to defend their territories from rivals.

According to the passage, which one of the following statements is correct?

A. Great Britain feeds more birds per capita than any other European nation.

B. The scientist's experiment was deemed incomplete because birdfeeders affected less than half of the birds studied.

C. Rival male birds rarely rely on birdfeeders for nourishment.

D. Birds that fast all night are more likely to rise and sing before sunrise.

24. Julius Caesar's first invasion of Britain, in 55 B.C., was unsuccessful, as he timed the attack in late summer and could not maintain the assault throughout the cold British winter. The second invasion, however, took place in the summer of 54 B.C. and comprised a much larger number of ships. In this campaign, Caesar's troops overwhelmed the most powerful tribes in the area and installed a new king that was friendly to the Roman Empire. The second conquest of Britain did not take place until 43 A.D., when Claudius reigned. After these battles, the Romans established a new capital at Camulodunum and maintained control of most of the British isles for the next three centuries.

According to the passage, which of the following is true?

A. British tribes could not defend themselves against an armed naval assault.

B. Caesar would have conquered Britain sooner if he knew more about the severity of its winter weather.

C. At some point between 54 B.C. and 43 A.D., the Roman Empire lost control of Britain.

D. The Roman control over Britain was more stable under Caligula's rule than under Caesar's.

25. Many modern naval vessels have been fitted with a sophisticated new sonar system called S2076 Stage 5. Environmentalists lament that the soundbursts emitted by the system, some of which exceed 250 decibels, are seriously damaging marine wildlife. To support this claim, they point to an extraordinary number of seal carcasses found washed up near areas where vessels have used S2076 Stage 5. The developers of this technology have responded by asserting that, although the number of seal deaths is unfortunate, no one has found a causal link between them and the use of S2076 Stage 5. They maintain that the system is safe.

The primary purpose of the passage is to

A. show that the environmentalists' accusations are false.

B. argue that use of S2076 should be discontinued.

C. emphasize the myriad threats humans pose to animals.

D. outline a controversy over the use of a new technology.

26. The most striking result of the expansion of social networking sites in the past few years has been the numerous legal questions regarding privacy policies. Some frustrated users have abandoned the sites over concerns that their information will be shared without their knowledge, while the sites' executives have insisted that they are constantly upgrading the tools users can employ to make sure what is private stays private. In the end, it seems unwise to assume that anything uploaded to a social networking site will remain unseen by those who are not permitted to see it. If you choose to post a picture on your page, make sure it's something you don't mind sharing with the world.

This passage is mainly about

A. how social networking sites and their users are struggling to find common ground when it comes to protecting personal content.

B. the startling drop in the number of people using social networking sites.

C. the need for regulators to intervene in a heated dispute.

D. the viability of social networking as an alternative to face-to-face relationships.

27. Although the most familiar type of spider web is called an "orb" web, some spiders make horizontal "funnel" webs in moist, sheltered places, such as under a rock or fallen tree. Underneath the flat sheet of web is a sequence of funnels that lead to a hole where the spider is concealed. When an insect strolls out onto the web's smooth surface, the spider senses the vibrations, emerges from the hole, bites the insect, and drags its meal back into the hole. Funnel webs are very durable, and spiders that construct them often build them for years.

From the passage above, it can be inferred that

A. funnel webs are less common than orb webs because they are more difficult to construct.

B. funnel-web spiders hunt mostly at night, when they are less visible.

C. if you see a funnel web, the spider inside has likely been around for a long time.

D. horizontal webs are more likely to trap insects than vertical ones are.

28. Ireland is known for its ancient castles that date back several centuries, to the time when most of the land was ruled by Vikings. Tourists can walk through their magnificent gardens and explore the majestic castles, many of which still have furniture and other antique items belonging to former residents. The Malahide Castle, located on the seaside of Dublin, Ireland's capital city, was home to members of the same family for more than 800 years.

Why does the writer mention Malahide Castle in the above paragraph?

A. To identify one of the most important Viking structures in Dublin.

B. To exemplify the age and historical significance of Dublin's ancient castles.

C. To describe the importance of maintaining ancient architecture for future generations to appreciate it.

D. To encourage tourists to assess the value of its antique furniture.

29. The ancient Chinese perspective regarding dragons is one that Americans might not expect. In America, dragons are typically portrayed as menacing and villainous monsters that crush villages, trample castles, and spew fiery breath at any hero who dares challenge them. In ancient China, however, these mythical beasts were wise, strong, compassionate, and protected people's families and land. Dragons were seen everywhere in ancient China—carved into temples, book covers, thrones, musical instruments, and weapons. In fact, the Chinese believed that their ruling class actually descended from dragons and continue to seek advice from them.

The author's main purpose is to

A. illustrate how two disparate cultures can still share beliefs.

B. reconcile contrary opinions of dragons.

C. identify a myth that overwhelmed an ancient culture.

D. emphasize the degree to which the ancient Chinese revered dragons.

30. Terra-cotta, or "baked earth," was originally used in architecture during the height of the Roman Empire. During the Renaissance, however, terra-cotta became a much more artistic medium. Many sculptors, for example, often used it to make *bozzetti*, or "rough drafts" of sculptures that would later be carved from stone or cast in bronze. Oddly enough, these *bozzetti* were often viewed as more interesting than the finished works, as art enthusiasts began collecting terra-cotta models for exhibition in their homes and in galleries. Collectors believed the models represented an artist's talent far more accurately. As a result, many of these "rough drafts" often commanded higher selling prices than the stone or bronze pieces on which they were based.

It can be inferred from the passage that terra-cotta was

A. so popular that collectors lost interest in finished sculptures.

B. just as sturdy a medium as stone or bronze.

C. easy for sculptors to acquire.

D. no longer used for architecture during the Renaissance.

PART IV

For the following ten questions, you will see two sentences. Read the sentences, and then choose the best answer to the question.

31. In recent years, the number of adults aged 18-24 without comprehensive health insurance has risen by 14%.

    Young adults are showing greater interest in extreme sports that threaten serious bodily injury.

    How are the two sentences related?

    A. They give the cause and effect of a trend.

    B. They create a problem and solution.

    C. They display a paradox.

    D. They reinforce each other.

32. Over the past several years, the state has seen an alarming rise in child obesity.

    The state government has enacted a tax on soft drinks, snacks, and other foods that contain more than a certain amount of sugar.

    What does the second sentence do?

    A. It suggests that the problem in the first sentence is unable to be solved.

    B. It presents a possible solution to the problem stated in the first sentence.

    C. It explains a reason for the problem stated in the first sentence.

    D. It repeats the sentiment that is implied by the first sentence.

33. Zebra mussels are filter feeders that cleanse freshwater lakes and therefore have helped increase the populations of smallmouth bass.

    Zebra mussel populations grow at an alarmingly fast rate, often dominating ecosystems to the detriment of other organisms.

    What does the second sentence do?

    A. It sums up the points made in the first sentence.

    B. It restates the opinion asserted in the first sentence.

    C. It provides contrary information.

    D. It gives an example for what is stated in the first sentence.

34. Over-the-counter medications are just as useful in combating head-cold symptoms as the medications that require a prescription.

    The cough syrup that I bought at the grocery store stopped my cough just as well as the expectorant I got from my pharmacist.

    How are the two sentences related?

    A. The second sentence provides an example of the conclusion asserted in the first.

    B. The second sentence shows there is no evidence to support the first.

    C. They restate the same information.

    D. They give a cause and its effect.

35. Consumer spending has dropped more than 30% over the past 12 months.

Unemployment has risen by 2.2% since this time last year.

What does the second sentence do?

A. It offers irrelevant information.

B. It offers a solution to a problem.

C. It states a potential cause.

D. It makes a comparison.

36. Specialists in early brain development believe that some video games can enhance a child's cognition and problem-solving ability.

Children under three who learn to solve simple jigsaw puzzles show a marked propensity to read sooner than those who do not.

What does the second sentence do?

A. It offers nothing relevant to support the first sentence.

B. It provides an alternate interpretation of the first sentence.

C. It contradicts the opinion given in the first sentence.

D. It reinforces the first sentence by offering similar evidence.

37. Because it was a holiday weekend, Marcus believed that the roads would be less crowded than usual.

That morning, Marcus chose to drive to the city rather than take public transportation.

What does the second sentence do?

A. It provides an application of the theory provided in the first sentence.

B. It contradicts the evidence given in the first sentence.

C. It presents a solution to the problem mentioned in the first sentence.

D. It repeats the same idea as stated in the first sentence.

38. Research indicates that male pattern baldness is genetic, passed from parent to child on the androgen receptor gene.

My father is bald, and lately I've noticed that my hairline is receding.

How are the two sentences related?

A. They create a contrast.

B. They provide a theory and a specific example.

C. They give a problem and a solution.

D. They repeat the same idea.

39. Many parents have withdrawn their children from private high schools because tuition costs have become prohibitively expensive.

   Over the past ten years, the median tuition price at private high schools has kept pace with the rate of increase in the cost of living index.

   How are the two sentences related?

   A. The second sentence provides supportive evidence for the first.

   B. They repeat the same idea.

   C. They provide a problem and a solution.

   D. The second analyzes the claim made in the first.

40. In order to stimulate spending, Congress authorized a rebate check for all individual taxpayers.

   When taxpayers received their rebate checks, they were more likely to save the money than to spend it.

   What does the second sentence do?

   A. It offers a potential cause.

   B. It states an unexpected consequence.

   C. It supports a conclusion.

   D. It exemplifies the first sentence.

PART V

ESSAY QUESTION:

"There is only one definition of success—to be able to spend your life in your own way."

To what extent do you agree with this statement? Explain your position by writing a unified essay using relevant reasons and/or examples from your own experience, observations, or reading.

ANSWER KEY—PRACTICE TEST 1

PART I

Question	Answer	Notes
1	C	
2	A	
3	D	
4	B	
5	D	
6	A	
7	C	
8	C	
9	B	
10	A	

PART II

Question	Answer	Notes
11	A	
12	C	
13	B	
14	A	
15	D	
16	B	
17	A	
18	A	
19	B	
20	D	

ANSWER KEY—PRACTICE TEST 1

PART III

Question	Answer	Notes
21	B	
22	B	
23	D	
24	C	
25	D	
26	A	
27	C	
28	B	
29	D	
30	C	

PART IV

Question	Answer	Notes
31	C	
32	B	
33	C	
34	A	
35	C	
36	D	
37	A	
38	B	
39	D	
40	B	

DETAILED ANSWERS—PRACTICE TEST 1

PART I

1.   This question is an example of an inverted sentence structure. Since the sentence begins with the negative phrase *never before*, the present perfect tense [*has* or *have*] plus the past participle, must be used. In addition, it's important to place the auxiliary verb *has* in front of the principal subject of the sentence, which is *mankind*. The answer is (C).

2.   The words *the one which he used to sail from Maine to Florida* are a dependent relative clause that cannot stand on its own as a complete sentence. Therefore, it needs to be set off by a comma. The answer is (A).

3.   The phrase *while walking through the woods* modifies *us*, since we were the ones who were walking. Therefore, the first word after the comma has to be "we." The best answer is (D).

4.   This question tests whether you can differentiate the subject pronoun *who* and the object pronoun *whom*. In this sentence, the person was taken to the prom and thus received the action; it was the brother who did the "taking." So the question should begin with *whom*. The best answer is (B).

5.   *Our museum owns a copy of The Mona Lisa* and *the original, however, is hanging in the Louvre* are complete sentences on their own. Therefore, it's OK to link them in the same sentence with a semicolon. Answer choices (A) and (B) have no punctuation separating the two phrases, and the comma in answer choice (C) creates a run-on sentence. The best answer is (D).

6.   In this sentence, the word *because* links *He was suspended from the team* and *he was late for too many practices*, but it serves as a subordinating conjunction, so it doesn't need a comma before it. The best answer is (A).

7.   When you compare two things, use the suffix *-er*, or the comparative form. If you are comparing three or more things, however, you must use the superlative form (*-est*). Since there are four moving trucks, the superlative form *largest* is correct. The best answer is (C).

8.   Whenever a speaker refers to himself in an imaginary situation—otherwise known as the subjunctive mood—the proper verb is *were* instead of *was*. The beginning of the sentence also needs to use *would*. The best answer is (C).

9.   Answer choice (A) is incorrect because it doesn't need *was* in the appositive (descriptive) clause. Answer choices (C) and (D) are incorrect because they are run-on sentences. *Perplexed by the tax forms* is a modifier that describes *Dennis*, so the best answer is (B).

10.   Punctuation should be enclosed within the final quotation mark when giving dialogue. Since this is a question, the sentence correctly has a question mark within the quotation marks. The best answer is (A).

PART II

11.   Sentences that use *not only* must also include *but also* to finish the parallel thought. The new sentence is *Jonathan is not only a great saxophone player but also a great trumpet player*. The best answer is (A).

12.   The new sentence is: *Having been delayed by traffic, she arrived at the airport too late to make her flight*. In the new sentence, the present participle phrase *Having been delayed in traffic* describes the woman that is the subject of the sentence. Therefore, *she* must come directly after the comma. Answer choice (B) is incorrect because it unnecessarily changes the verb tense from the simple past. The best answer is (C).

13.   The new sentence is: *I was nervous when the park ranger warned me about bears in the national park*. The word *when* forms a subordinate clause in the second part of the new sentence, and there is no need to change the verb tense from the simple past in both parts of the sentence. The best answer is (B).

14.   The new sentence is: *He will only buy the car if he receives financing from his bank*. This is a conditional sentence that states that one thing (getting financing) has to happen first, in the present tense, in order for the other (buying the car) to happen in the future tense. The best answer is (A).

15. The new sentence is: *The road was blocked off from all car traffic because it was flooded by the massive rainstorm.* The flooding caused the road to be blocked off, so you can use *because* in order to link the two clauses. And the sentence should stay consistently in the simple past tense. The best answer is (D).

16. *Because of* links the two phrases in the sentence together, and it needs to be followed by a noun phrase. Therefore, the simple past tense *refused* in the initial sentence must be changed to its noun form, *refusal*. The best answer is (B).

17. The new sentence compares Spanish and Italian and asserts that the two are not like each other. The phrase *Unlike Italian* modifies *Spanish*, so *Spanish* must come directly after the comma. The best answer is (A).

18. The new sentence will be: *If it snows, the city's sanitation will work overtime.* The phrase *in the event of* should be followed by a noun or noun phrase, but *If* is followed by a simple present tense. The best answer is (A).

19. The new sentence would be constructed as follows: *If he had finished his final exams, he would have been able to go to the beach.* The new construction is conditional, and since he didn't go the beach, the conclusion is an imaginary situation that requires *would*. The best answer is (B).

20. The new sentence would be constructed as follows: *Although he attempted it many times, he was unable to ride the bull for more than five seconds.* The second half of the sentence is unchanged, but the first must change because *despite* takes a noun phrase and *although* takes a simple subject and verb. The best answer is (D).

PART III

21. The passage introduces us to the CRRNJ and describes how it grew over the latter half of the 19th century. It doesn't provide a comprehensive history, because it's very difficult to provide a complete and detailed history in only five sentences. Answer choices (C) and (D) are never mentioned. The best answer is (B).

22.   The passage starts by discussing a problem and then mentions a study that has helped lead to a solution to that problem. Therefore, the writer believes that if another similar cloud occurs, it might not be as big a problem because people will be better equipped to analyze it. The information in answer choices (A), (C), and (D) is not stated in the passage. The best answer is (B).

23.   The experiment in the passage details how birds that eat during the night tend to rise later in the day, so it stands to reason that those who fast all night get up earlier in order to eat something in their natural environment and sing before sunrise to attract females. The best answer is (D).

24.   The passage states that Caesar conquered Britain in 54 B.C. and refers to a second conquest in 43 A.D. If the Romans saw fit to invade Britain again, it must be true that they lost control of Britain between those two dates. Answer choice (B) might seem possible, but we don't know that the only thing keeping Caesar from conquering Britain was the weather. Other factors might have been involved. The best answer is (C).

25.   The passage describes the use of S2076 Stage 5 and provides both sides of the argument over whether it should be used. The author does not reveal his opinion either way, so answer choices (A), (B), and (C) are far too extreme and one-sided. The best answer is (D).

26.   The passage asserts that some users don't like their perceived lack of privacy when it comes to using social networking sites, and that the sites are trying to reassure users that their content is not under threat. The best answer is (A).

27.   The last sentence in the passage states that *spiders that construct [funnel webs] often build them for years*. This means that any funnel web you come across probably took a long time to make, so you can infer that the spider has likely been in that location for a while. The best answer is (C).

28.   The main idea of the paragraph is that Ireland (and more specifically, Dublin) has several ancient castles that preserve an idea of what life was like several centuries ago. Malahide Castle is referenced as an example of one such castle, which dates back 800 years. (Note that *exemplify* means "to give an example.") The best answer is (B).

29. The passage discusses several ways in which the ancient Chinese people revered (or "looked up to") dragons, but it does nothing to reconcile the views of Chinese and American cultures, nor does it indicate that dragons overwhelmed the culture. The best answer is (D).

30. The passage states that *many sculptors often* used terra-cotta to make these rough drafts, so it's unlikely that terra-cotta would be in such broad use if it were expensive or rare. The best answer is (C).

PART IV

31. If young adults do not have health insurance, one might expect that they would avoid subjecting themselves to getting hurt. However, the second sentence asserts the exact opposite idea, thus displaying a paradox, or two situations that seem to contradict each other. The best answer is (C).

32. The problem is the increasing numbers of children who suffer from obesity. The proposed solution is to levy a tax on the sugary foods that children eat, in order to discourage people from buying them. The best answer is (B).

33. The first sentence suggests that zebra mussels are helpful to other species in the water they inhabit, but the second sentence provides information that suggests that the mussels are hurtful. In other words, the second contradicts (or "says the opposite of") the first one. The best answer is (C).

34. The cough syrup in sentence 2 is an example of an over-the-counter medication referenced in sentence 1. They don't restate the same information, however, since the first sentence is far more general than the second one. The best answer is (A).

35. The first sentence states that people aren't spending as much money as they normally do, and the first provides a possible reason by stating that more people have lost their jobs over the same time period. The best answer is (C).

36. Both sentences talk about the positive effects of games and puzzles on the early development of a child's brain. So the second sentence reinforces the idea proposed in the first. The best answer is (D).

37. Marcus had a theory that there wouldn't be as much traffic on the roads, and he applied this theory by driving rather than taking public transportation. The sentences don't contradict each other, and there is no problem to solve. The best answer is (A).

38. The first sentence states a theory based on research, and the second sentence is more specific, as it relates to two particular people. Answer choice (D) is incorrect, because although the sentences clearly support each other, they do not repeat the same idea. The best answer is (B).

39. The first sentence states a claim among parents that it has become too expensive to educate their children in a private high school, and the second sentence analyzes that claim by stating that prices at private high schools have increased at the same rate as everything else. The best answer is (D).

40. Congress wanted people to spend the money it gave taxpayers, but they saved it instead. So this result was something Congress did not expect. The best answer is (B).

PART V

Here is a sample response to the essay question:

> When people are asked to define success, I think most say that success depends on how much money you've earned. I have to disagree, however, because I believe success is based on happiness, which has nothing to do with money. I've known richer people than me who are miserable, and I've known poorer people than me without a care in the world. Happiness comes from being comfortable in your own skin, and by living the life you want. These are the people who have found the most success, and that's why, for the following three reasons, I agree with the given essay prompt.
>
> I don't come from a very rich family. My dad repairs telephone equipment and my mom is a nurse, and neither of them makes a lot of money. And despite the many challenges of raising four kids in a middle-class household, my parents seem very happy. My dad always

said he wanted to work outdoors instead of behind a desk, and my mom told me she has wanted to care for sick people since she was seven years old. In these respects, they have succeeded in finding careers that fit with the goals they set.

Conversely, my friend Jeff's family has a lot more money than mine does, yet he never sees his father because he's always working or traveling around the world. Last month Jeff scored the winning goal in a lacrosse playoff game, and his dad couldn't attend because he was working in Istanbul. I've talked to Jeff's dad about careers, and he says he is stuck between liking the law and disliking being a lawyer. He enjoys researching and arguing cases, but hates that he has to spend so much time away from his family to do it. Clearly, Jeff's dad is not as successful as he might seem. What good is a lot of money if it takes you away from the people you love?

Jeff's dad reminds me of William Foster Kane, the wealthy newspaper publisher in one of my favorite movies, <u>Citizen Kane</u>. Kane amasses amazing wealth, yet he dies alone in a mansion full of possessions he never enjoyed, longing for his favorite childhood sled. The movie is a fictional story, but I think it depicts a very compelling real-life scenario where people place too much value on the money they earn, at the expense of the personal relationships that give life it's most profound meaning.

In conclusion, I believe the best way to measure your success is to figure out how happy you are to get out of bed in the morning. It is way too common in our materialistic lifestyle to let your possessions show the world what a "success" you are. But believe that if you have a job you like, a family around you, and a way to balance your life between them, you can look in the mirror and see a successful person staring back.

Accuplacer

Practice Test 2

ANSWER SHEET—PRACTICE TEST 2

PART I

1. Ⓐ Ⓑ Ⓒ Ⓓ
2. Ⓐ Ⓑ Ⓒ Ⓓ
3. Ⓐ Ⓑ Ⓒ Ⓓ

4. Ⓐ Ⓑ Ⓒ Ⓓ
5. Ⓐ Ⓑ Ⓒ Ⓓ
6. Ⓐ Ⓑ Ⓒ Ⓓ

7. Ⓐ Ⓑ Ⓒ Ⓓ
8. Ⓐ Ⓑ Ⓒ Ⓓ

9. Ⓐ Ⓑ Ⓒ Ⓓ
10. Ⓐ Ⓑ Ⓒ Ⓓ

PART II

11. Ⓐ Ⓑ Ⓒ Ⓓ _____
12. Ⓐ Ⓑ Ⓒ Ⓓ _____
13. Ⓐ Ⓑ Ⓒ Ⓓ _____
14. Ⓐ Ⓑ Ⓒ Ⓓ _____
15. Ⓐ Ⓑ Ⓒ Ⓓ _____
16. Ⓐ Ⓑ Ⓒ Ⓓ _____
17. Ⓐ Ⓑ Ⓒ Ⓓ _____
18. Ⓐ Ⓑ Ⓒ Ⓓ _____
19. Ⓐ Ⓑ Ⓒ Ⓓ _____
20. Ⓐ Ⓑ Ⓒ Ⓓ _____

PART III

21. Ⓐ Ⓑ Ⓒ Ⓓ
22. Ⓐ Ⓑ Ⓒ Ⓓ
23. Ⓐ Ⓑ Ⓒ Ⓓ

24. Ⓐ Ⓑ Ⓒ Ⓓ
25. Ⓐ Ⓑ Ⓒ Ⓓ
26. Ⓐ Ⓑ Ⓒ Ⓓ

27. Ⓐ Ⓑ Ⓒ Ⓓ
28. Ⓐ Ⓑ Ⓒ Ⓓ

29. Ⓐ Ⓑ Ⓒ Ⓓ
30. Ⓐ Ⓑ Ⓒ Ⓓ

PART IV

31. Ⓐ Ⓑ Ⓒ Ⓓ
32. Ⓐ Ⓑ Ⓒ Ⓓ
33. Ⓐ Ⓑ Ⓒ Ⓓ

34. Ⓐ Ⓑ Ⓒ Ⓓ
35. Ⓐ Ⓑ Ⓒ Ⓓ
36. Ⓐ Ⓑ Ⓒ Ⓓ

37. Ⓐ Ⓑ Ⓒ Ⓓ
38. Ⓐ Ⓑ Ⓒ Ⓓ

39. Ⓐ Ⓑ Ⓒ Ⓓ
40. Ⓐ Ⓑ Ⓒ Ⓓ

ANSWER SHEET

PART V

_____

_____

_____

_____

_____

_____

_____

_____

_____

_____

_____

_____

_____

_____

PART I

Select the best substitute for the underlined parts of the following ten sentences. The first answer [choice A] is identical to the original sentence. If you think the original sentence is best, then choose A as your answer.

1. Skating past the last defender, <u>my father saw me score</u> the game-winning goal.

    A. my father saw me score

    B. my father saw me having scored

    C. I scored

    D. I was scoring

2. <u>Possession of a handgun without a permit</u> is illegal in many states.

    A. Possession of a handgun without a permit

    B. When you possess a handgun without a permit, it

    C. Possessing a handgun without a permit, this

    D. When you possess of a handgun without a permit

3. I can run faster than my brother, even though he is three <u>years older than me.</u>

    A. years older than me.

    B. years older than I.

    C. years' older than I.

    D. years' older than myself.

4. Despite my lingering fears, <u>my son got my permission to drive the day he</u> <u>earned his driver's license.</u>

    A. my son got my permission to drive the day he earned his driver's license.

    B. my son was permitted to drive on the day he earned his driver's license.

    C. I permitted my son to drive my car the day he earned his driver's license.

    D. on the day my son earned his driver's license, I permitted him to drive my car.

5. The prosecuting attorney asked the <u>witness "Where were you on the night the</u> <u>crime was committed"?</u>

    A. witness "Where were you on the night the crime was committed"?

    B. witness, "Where were you on the night the crime was committed?"

    C. witness. "Where were you on the night the crime was committed?"

    D. witness: "Where were you on the night the crime was committed"?

6. Whenever I go to the <u>library, I try to remember to bring</u> the books I've already borrowed.

    A. library, I try to remember to bring

    B. library I tried to remember bringing

    C. library, I am trying to remember bringing

    D. library, I had tried to remember whether I brought

7. In the northern Aleutian Islands, many indigenous native tribes are able to live comfortably <u>in spite of having a colder climate than anywhere</u> on the planet.

    A. in spite of having a colder climate than anywhere

    B. in spite of having a colder climate

C. despite of having the colder climate than anywhere

D. despite having one of the coldest climates

8. I tried to dunk the <u>basketball however the rim was</u> too high.

A. basketball however the rim was

B. basketball, the rim was however

C. basketball. The rim, however, was

D. basketball; the rim was however

9. <u>Having a good product and to deliver it efficiently are the keys</u> to a successful business.

A. Having a good product and to deliver it efficiently are the keys

B. To have a good product and delivering it efficiently is key

C. A good product and to deliver it efficiently is the key

D. A good product and an efficient way to deliver it are the keys

10. No sooner <u>had school ended for the summer when the children were running</u> into the playground, jumping for joy.

A. had school ended for the summer when the children were running

B. had school ended for the summer than the children ran

C. school had ended for the summer than the children ran

D. was school ending for the summer when the children were running

PART II

Rewrite the following ten sentences mentally in your own head. Follow the directions given for the formation of the new sentence. Remember that your new sentence should be grammatically correct and convey the same meaning as the original sentence.

11. Jeffrey ran for his gate as soon as he passed through the airline security station.

Rewrite, using: <u>Once he</u>

The next words will be:

A. was passing

B. had passed

C. had been passing

D. will pass

12. Blessed with consistently pleasant weather, Hawaii is a common destination for honeymooners.

Rewrite, beginning with: <u>Hawaii</u>

Your new sentence will include:

A. because it had been

B. because being

C. because of it being

D. because it is

13. The zookeepers, who worried that the escaped cobra would bite them, were reluctant to enter the reptile house.

Rewrite, beginning with: <u>The zookeepers were</u>

Your new sentence will include:

A. so they were

B. and that they were

C. but they did

D. because they had

14. As he drove to his sister's house, Paul listened to an audio book on his car stereo.

Rewrite, beginning with: <u>Driving</u>

Your new sentence will include:

A. house Paul was listening

B. house, and Paul listened

C. house, Paul listened

D. house that Paul listened

15. Even though the economy shows signs of improving, housing prices continue to fall.

Rewrite, beginning with: <u>Despite</u>

The next words will be:

A. the economy

B. signs that

C. housing prices

D. improving economy

16. If he were taller, he would try to play professional basketball.

Rewrite, beginning with: <u>He cannot play</u>

Your new sentence will include:

A. although he can

B. because he is not

C. despite his inability to

D. instead of his ability to

17. Most political candidates reach out beyond their political base when they announce their candidacy for president.

Rewrite, beginning with: <u>Reaching out</u>

Your new sentence will include:

A. is normality of political candidates

B. is normal among political candidates

C. normal political candidate's

D. normality with political candidates

18. Americans have not suffered as much collective grief as they did the day John F. Kennedy was assassinated.

Rewrite, beginning with: <u>Never again</u>

The next words will be:

A. will Americans suffer

B. have Americans suffered

C. do Americans suffer

D. can the grief of Americans

19. He was ecstatic because he was able to adopt a child after so many years of waiting.

Rewrite, beginning with: <u>He waited many years</u>

The next words will be:

A. of adopting

B. ecstatically

C. to adopt

D. in ecstasy

20. Atlanta, like many other new American cities, doubled in size in only its first ten years of existence.

Rewrite, beginning with: <u>As</u>

The next words will be:

A. were

B. had

C. was

D. did

PART III

For the following ten questions, read the passage and then select the correct answer to the question. You may need to answer based on explicit information from the passage, as well as ideas that are suggested or implied in the passage.

21. No other country has more profound lingual diversity than China, whose 1.3 billion inhabitants fall within eight major linguistic groups. Mainland academics may argue that all Chinese people are linked by the universal characters of written Chinese, but this assertion fails to address the simple fact that these eight localized spoken dialects, though related, are mutually incomprehensible. And despite many attempts to create a standardized spoken Chinese language, or guoyu, provincial loyalties have scuttled the effort every time.

    According to this passage, the most consistent obstacle to a unified Chinese language is

    A. political uncertainty

    B. government ineptitude

    C. regional pride

    D. subpar education

22. Thomas, a high school senior from State A, expressed an interest in attending Edison State College, which is located in State B. After a little research, Thomas's parents discovered that children of residents of State B pay substantially less for tuition at Edison State than do children of out-of-state residents. Using this information, Thomas's parents decided to move to State B. And when Thomas enrolled at Edison State the following fall, his parents' in-state status allowed them to save a lot of money on their tuition payments.

    We can conclude from the information in the passage that

    A. in order to qualify for the lower tuition, applicants need not prove they have lived in State B for more than one year.

    B. Thomas's parents did not apply for a scholarship due to financial need.

C. Edison State's tuition is among the lowest of all colleges in State B.

D. There are no colleges in State A that offer similar tuition discounts to in-state residents.

23. Public health officials are becoming concerned about chlorine, a chemical that is added to many municipal water supplies to reduce bacterial growth. New evidence shows that the rate of a first-trimester miscarriage is increased significantly when a pregnant woman drinks five or more glasses of chlorinated water per day. Lead, which has been shown to cause brain damage in small children, is another main contaminant in urban water systems. Rising fears about these and other problems—such as toxic bacteria, cysts, and algae—have caused an increase in the number of alternate methods of water filtration that are available to the general public.

The passage is chiefly concerned with

A. offering background information regarding heightened interest in safe water

B. creating fear over problems that cannot be solved

C. enumerating the many potential dangers that pregnant women encounter

D. urging people to find alternate sources of hydration

24. One of the greatest intellectual breakthroughs of the 20th century was the discovery that the universe is constantly expanding. It is difficult to fathom, however, why this revelation took so long to discover, since Isaac Newton and his colleagues should have known that gravity would cause an inert universe ultimately to shrink. Further study could have helped physicists determine the minimal rate at which the universe must be growing, in order to compensate for the gravitational forces holding it back. Instead, the theory of a static universe persisted centuries after Newton's death.

The author of the passage mentions Isaac Newton in order to

A. provide evidence that the universe is shrinking

B. support the idea that physicists should have proved the static universe theory false long before they did

C. illustrate how revered he was in the fields of astronomy and physics

D. show the ramifications of widespread ignorance among scientific professionals

25. Domesticated cats and dogs both see their human owners as pseudoparents, but for different reasons. Cats develop a bond with their masters early in life, when they respond to the food and comfort given to them by their human guardians. Dogs, by contrast, view their masters through the lens of their innate pack mentality, which confers on the human a very important status relationship. This is why, when they leave the house, the cat runs off to explore independently, while the dog's innate response is to look back to find packmates with which to roam.

The primary purpose of the passage is to:

A. lament the enmity cats and dogs feel for each other

B. advocate that different animals make better pets for different people

C. draw a particular contrast between cats and dogs

D. criticize dogs for their inborn dependency on others

26. Although jazz is mostly an improvisational form, it is easy to detect from its exotic sound its many disparate musical roots. The fundamental syncopation and the common inclusion of a piano and brass instruments—such as the cornet, trumpet, and trombone—suggest the influence of ragtime. The subsequent addition of saxophones stems from the debt jazz owes to dance orchestras. Brass bands were also one of the chief inspirations of jazz's ensemble mentality, whereby all musicians play lead and counter melodies simultaneously. But the most striking features of jazz originate directly from the blues, where musical soloists often mimic the vocals while distorting them using various unique effects.

This passage is mainly about:

A. the influence of blues on the uniquely American form of jazz

B. the complexity of jazz's many musical forebears

C. comparing the relative merits of several unique musical forms

D. the versatility of various musical instruments

27. While comparing economic data, a group of sociologists concluded that, among all people at a certain income level, individuals in rural areas have greater purchasing power than those living in urban or suburban regions. The group factored in several data points, including the population density within a certain radius of city centers, the number of people per household, and the percentage of those households that included two working parents. Ultimately, however, the main premise was that the money spent by urban and suburban dwellers on their fundamental need for food and shelter could be spent by rural households on discretionary items.

From the passage above, it can be inferred that

A. Rural households spend less on food and housing than either urban or sub-urban households do.

B. The average urban or suburban household contains fewer people than the average rural household.

C. Suburban households have more purchasing power than urban house-holds.

D. The farther away from a city center, the less purchasing power a rural household has.

28. In the early 20th century, it was theorized that ice ages resulted from variations in the Earth's orbit. No one could attempt to prove this theory, however, because there was not enough trustworthy data about when ice ages occurred and how long they lasted. Recently, however, a group of scientists discovered how to determine this chronology by using two oxygen isotopes, 16 and 18, that are found in ocean residue. Almost all oxygen in ocean water is oxygen 16, but the forming of ice sheets results in less water evaporating from the ocean, and an increasing ratio of oxygen 18 molecules. The greater the ratio of these heavier molecules found in ocean sediments, the more land ice was present.

The author of this passage is primarily interested in

A. initiating debate on a theory that many believe to be flawed

B. decrying how research can often be undermined by the lack of sufficient data

C. presenting a conjecture and a new way to test its validity

D. attempting to resolve a heated controversy

29. With the advent of the Internet, it is now widely believed that the most successful corporate managers are those who deviate from classical management models. Whereas before it was important to determine and weigh all options, a process often delayed by bureaucracy and an inability to find consensus, now most successful managers say they rely on "intuition." This is not, as many people believe, advocating uninformed impulses when making decisions, but rather a very specific impulse sharpened by years of experience and practice. In many cases, this particular style of thinking can expose flaws in tried-and-true methods that have not evolved with the times and are therefore inadequate on their own.

It can be inferred from the passage that successful managers

A. adhere to strict regimens of thought when formulating solutions

B. cannot justify their instinctual decisions to those with less experience

C. use their practical experience to develop a specific feel that can vary from case to case

D. are no better off now than before the Internet became so commonplace

30. From 1910 to 1930, more than ten percent of the African-American population in southern American states moved northward, presumably to meet the increased labor demand in many northern cities. It had been widely assumed that most of these workers came from rural areas, but in fact more than a third of them were engaged in skilled trades before they left the South. It may seem curious that such a significant percentage of securely employed people would migrate northward, but in truth workers' conditions in the South were declining rapidly at the time. Therefore, most of these participants in the Great Migration were not enticed by the opportunity to live a more urban lifestyle, but rather by the simple promise of higher wages and a more secure standard of living.

The primary purpose of this passage is to

A. explain away data that the author feels are irrelevant

B. challenge a widely accepted explanation

C. urge readers to reassess an unjustly discarded theory

D. introduce a recently unearthed data source

PART IV

For the following ten questions, you will see two sentences. Read the sentences, and then choose the best answer to the question.

31. Now is the perfect time to buy a home, because housing prices in Essex County are so low.

    Property taxes in Essex County have recently risen to a 10-year high.

    What does the second sentence do?

    A. It states an effect.

    B. It undermines the first.

    C. It repeats information.

    D. It provides an example.

32. Over the past two months, the average price of a gallon of gasoline in Johnson County has risen 15%.

    Over that same time period, Johnson County gas station owners reported a 12% increase in gasoline sales.

    What does the second sentence do?

    A. It corroborates the data given in the first sentence.

    B. It states the effect.

    C. It is unrelated to the first sentence.

    D. It provided unexpected information.

33. Health professionals argue that too much butter in a person's diet increases the chance of a heart attack.

    In South Korea, where per-capita consumption of butter is very low, heart attacks are no less prevalent than in countries where butter is served at every meal.

    How are the two sentences related?

    A. They contradict each other.

    B. The second sentence shows there is no evidence to support the first.

    C. They state the same information.

    D. They state a problem and a solution.

34. Voters are poised to reject the referendum for spending municipal taxes to build a new baseball stadium.

    If the new stadium is not built, the local team's owner has threatened to move his franchise.

    What does the second sentence do?

    A. It provides analysis from a different perspective.

    B. It offers a solution to a problem.

    C. It states a potential consequence.

    D. It contradicts the first sentence.

35. Health advocates are worried about a growth hormone used on livestock that increases the ratio of meat to fat.

Physicians say humans can safely ingest 15 milligrams of lipazine per day, and no animals ever receive a dose greater than 10 milligrams.

How are the two sentences related?

A. One provides an application of the theory expressed in the first.

B. The second sentence attempts to address a problem presented in the first sentence.

C. They provide a problem and a consequence of that problem.

D. They provide identical information.

36. Attendance at a local indoor health club has recently risen sharply.

Over the past month, our weather has been unseasonably cold and rainy.

What does the second sentence do?

A. It makes a comparison.

B. It provides an application for a theory.

C. It states an unexpected consequence.

D. It states a potential cause.

37. Glaucoma, an eye-related disease among Americans over 50 years old, will become a bigger problem in the near future.

The median age of all Americans will likely reach 50 within five years.

What does the second sentence do?

A. It provides a contrast to the first sentence.

B. It provides evidence for the first sentence.

C. It is unrelated to the first sentence.

D. It repeats the same idea as stated in the first sentence.

38. Polls indicate that many Americans do not reveal all of their income on their income tax returns.

My uncle received a cash settlement and neglected to pay tax on it.

How are these sentences related?

A. They create a contrast.

B. They provide a theory and a specific example.

C. They provide an explanation for a contentious topic.

D. The second analyzes a claim made in the first.

39. Movies that are rated "R" usually dramatize scenes of extreme violence and are thus restricted to children aged 17 or over.

Many children under 17 years of age routinely witness violent scenes on television.

What does the second sentence do?

A. It provides irrelevant information.

B. It substantiates a claim made in the first sentence.

C. It refutes the first sentence.

D. It states the effect.

40. In 2011, the legislature of State B introduced an unpopular bill that effectively revoked the collective bargaining rights of public-sector labor unions.

The governor asserted that this change was necessary in order to balance the state's budget.

What does the second sentence do?

A. It states an unexpected consequence.

B. It refutes the claim cited in the first sentence.

C. It provides an explanation for a contentious topic.

D. It restates the information given in the first sentence.

PART V

ESSAY QUESTION:

"The people we remember best are the ones who broke the rules."

To what extent do you agree with this statement? Explain your position by writing a unified essay using relevant reasons and/or examples from your own experience, observations, or reading.

ANSWER KEY—PRACTICE TEST 2

PART I

Question	Answer	Notes
1	C	
2	A	
3	B	
4	C	
5	B	
6	A	
7	D	
8	C	
9	D	
10	B	

PART II

Question	Answer	Notes
11	B	
12	D	
13	A	
14	C	
15	B	
16	B	
17	B	
18	A	
19	C	
20	D	

ANSWER KEY—PRACTICE TEST 2

PART III

Question	Answer	Notes
21	C	
22	A	
23	A	
24	B	
25	C	
26	B	
27	A	
28	C	
29	C	
30	B	

PART IV

Question	Answer	Notes
31	B	
32	D	
33	A	
34	C	
35	B	
36	D	
37	B	
38	B	
39	A	
40	C	

DETAILED ANSWERS—PRACTICE TEST 2

PART I

1.   The way this question is set up, the opening phrase *Skating past the last defender* modifies *my father*, even though the author is the one who is playing hockey. This is a misplaced modifier, so answer choices (A) and (B) can be eliminated. Answer choices (C) and (D) correct this problem, but (D) is in the wrong tense. The simple past tense is correct, and thus the best answer is (C).

2.   The sentence is correct as written, because the noun form *Possession* is a stronger subject than *When you possess*, and it agrees with the verb *is*. Also, answer choices (C) and (D) have improper sentence structure; in (C) the *this* and the comma are unnecessary, and (D) does not have a clear subject. The best answer is (A).

3.   This question tests the proper use of pronouns. The two brothers are being compared, and as the sentence is written, the subject pronoun *he* does not agree with the object pronoun *me*. Therefore, answer choice (A) is incorrect. For similar reasons, you can eliminate answer choice (D). Answer choices (B) and (C) correct this error, but (C) includes the unnecessary possessive *years'*. The best answer is (B).

4.   The opening phrase *Despite my lingering fears* refers to the author of the sentence, so the first noun after the comma should be *I*, not *my son*. Therefore, you can eliminate answer choices (A), (B), and (D). The best answer is (C).

5.   The first issue in this sentence involves the punctuation involved in quotations. The two main points are that a comma should precede an opening quotation mark, and that the question mark should be within the closing quotation mark. Therefore, the best answer is (B).

6.   This sentence is written correctly, because it maintains the present tense established by the opening phrase *Whenever I go*. It also uses the proper idiom *remember … to*. Answer choice (B) changes the verb to the past tense, (C) misuses the idiom, and (D) changes the verb to the past perfect tense. The best answer is (A).

7.   Don't be thrown by whether to use *despite* or *in spite of*, since the two are inter-changeable. The real issue is the comparative *colder climate*; the sentence is incorrectly written because it should say *than anywhere **else***. Otherwise, the climate would have to be colder than itself, which is impossible. Eliminate answer choices (A) and (C). Answer choice (B) is incorrect because *colder* needs *than*. The best answer is (D).

8.   This question tests the proper use of the word *however*. As written, the sentence is a run-on, and a comma doesn't solve the problem. Since the two clauses are independent (they could survive on their own as complete sentences), you need a semi-colon or a period to separate them. Therefore, the best answer is (C).

9.   This sentence has two subjects (the *product* and the *delivery*), so a parallel construction requires that the sentence use the plural *keys*. After you eliminate answer choices (B) and (C), you can also get rid of answer choice (A) because the structure is not parallel; *Having a product* does not match the tense of *to deliver*. The best answer is (D).

10.   This question is an example of the inverted sentence structure. When a sentence begins with a negative phrase like *No sooner*, you should use the past perfect *had ... ended*. In addition, the auxiliary verb *had* must be placed *in front of school*, which is the subject of the sentence. Therefore, the best answer is (B).

PART II

11.   The new sentence is: *Once he had passed through the airline security station, Jeffrey ran for his gate*. The construction *once* uses the past perfect tense, and the best answer is (B).

12.   The new sentence is: *Hawaii is a common destination for honeymooners because it is blessed with consistently pleasant weather*. The other answer choices use an incorrect verb tense, so the best answer is (D).

13.   The new sentence isn't all that different from the original: *The zookeepers were worried that the escaped cobra would bite them, so they were reluctant to enter the reptile house*. The best answer is (A).

14. The new sentence is: *Driving to his sister's house, Paul listened to an audio book on his car stereo.* There is no need to change the verb tense, so the best answer is (C).

15. This one can seem tricky, because you have to decide which noun appears first in the sentence. This new sentence reads: *Despite signs that the economy is improving, housing prices continue to fall.* Note that another possible construction is *Despite signs of economic improvement*, but that isn't an option among the answer choices. The best answer is (B).

16. The new sentence is: *He cannot play professional basketball because he is not taller.* The best answer is (B).

17. The new sentence creates a new subject, *Reaching*, so the proper verb to go with it is *is*. The new sentence is: *Reaching out beyond their political base is normal among political candidates when they announce their candidacy for president.* The best answer is (B). (I know! Three B's in a row. Weird, right?)

18. This is another often-used inversion structure, and your job is to switch the sentence around, like this: *Never again will Americans suffer as much collective grief as they did the day John F. Kennedy was assassinated.* The best answer is (A).

19. The new sentence starts with *He waited many years to adopt a child* because idiomatically, *waiting* goes with the preposition *to*. The best answer is (C).

20. The new sentence retains the comparison, but instead of comparing cities, the new sentence compares the actual process of doubling. The new sentence looks like this: *As did many other new American cities, Atlanta doubled in size in only its first ten years of existence.* The best answer is (D).

PART III

21. The last sentence of the passage mentions that "despite many attempts to create a standardized spoken Chinese language . . . *provincial loyalties* have scuttled the effort every time." This is a nice paraphrase for "regional pride." None of the other answer choices is mentioned, and the best answer is (C).

22. This is an inference question, so the key is to ask yourself what must be true. And we know that answer choice (A) is true, because if it weren't Thomas would not have been eligible to receive the discounted tuition. We don't know whether they *needed* to save the money; they could have chosen to. So answer choice (B) is out. We know nothing about answer choices (C) or (D), either. The best answer is (A).

23. This passage is chiefly concerned with listing a number of potential dangers in drinking water. Answer choice (B) is too strong, because even though we don't know whether the problems can be solved, we do know people are looking to solve them. Answer choice (C) is too specific, as it only deals with the one sentence about pregnant women. And answer choice (D) is too strong, because there is no advocacy involved. The best answer is (A).

24. The passage says that "theory of a static universe persisted centuries after Newton's death," indicating that he lived long before the "discovery that the universe is constantly expanding" in the 20th century. The author therefore mentions Newton to indicate that he could have come up with the idea long before it actually came to pass. The best answer is (B).

25. Answer choices (A), (B), and (D) are too extreme, because they mention feelings that just don't appear in the passage. We don't know if dogs and cats hate each other, or which, if any, the author prefers. The passage is merely a neutral list of ways in which dogs and cats are different, and the best answer is (C).

26. Answer choice (A) is too narrow, because even though the passage states that "the most striking features of jazz originate directly from the blues," that isn't the subject of the whole passage. The author never compares the influencing styles. And although lots of musical instruments are mentioned, nothing about their versatility is mentioned. The best answer is (B).

27. This is another tricky inference question. The passage says that "individuals in rural areas have greater purchasing power than those living in urban or suburban regions," mainly because "the money spent by urban and suburban dwellers on their fundamental need for food and shelter could be spent by rural households on discretionary items." That is a long and complicated way of saying that rural dwellers pay less for food and shelter. The best answer is (A).

28. In the passage, the conjecture (another word for "theory") is that "ice ages resulted from variations in the Earth's orbit." And now there is a new way to test this chronology, using those two oxygen isotopes. There is no debate or controversy over the theory, so answer choices (A) and (D) are out. Although there wasn't enough information initially, the author's point is that there is now. The best answer is (C).

29. This passage is about a revised definition of "intuition," which is "a very specific impulse sharpened by years of experience and practice." They specifically do not adhere to strict regimens of anything, so you can get rid of answer choice (A). Answer choice (B) is never mentioned, and answer choice (D) is irrelevant. The best answer is (C).

30. In this case, the theory that the author mentions is "widely assumed"—which means the same things as "widely accepted"—and the author wants to challenge it. The author doesn't mention any data that he perceives to be irrelevant. The theory has not been discarded, unjustly or otherwise, so you can eliminate answer choice (C). And although the conclusion is new, the data source is not. So you can get rid of (D) as well. The best answer is (B).

PART IV

31. The first sentence says it's a good time to buy a home because prices are low, but the second states the opposite (or undermines it) by saying the tax you'll pay on that new house is higher than ever. The best answer is (B).

32. Given the first sentence's claim that gas prices are rising, you might expect gas consumption to go down. The assertion that it, too, is increasing is unexpected. The best answer is (D).

33. The first sentence states evidence that butter is bad for you, yet the second statement says Koreans have the same problems and eat hardly any butter at all—implying that maybe the heart problems are caused by something else. The two statements contradict each other and the best answer is (A).

34. In the first sentence, we learn that it is unlikely that voters will support a new stadium, and the second sentence tells us what might happen if the stadium is not built. The second sentence is a potential consequence of the first, and the best answer is (C).

35. In the first sentence, health advocates express worry that a growth hormone used on livestock is unsafe for humans. The second aims to soothe those worries by saying the dosage is too small for humans to be affected. The best answer is (B).

36. The first sentence states a fact, that more people are working out indoors. The second tries to explain that fact by saying the weather outside is terrible. The best answer is (D).

37. The first sentence says that glaucoma affects people over 50, and it makes sense that the disease will be a bigger problem if there are more 50-year-olds in the world. The second statement supports the first with extra evidence, and the best answer is (B).

38. The first statement is a theory that Americans do not reveal all of their income on their income tax returns, and the second sentence supports that theory by providing evidence of one particular person doing just that. The best answer is (B).

39. The first statement talks about children over 17 and movies, whereas the second talks about kids that are under 17 and television. The second does not address anything specific; it especially doesn't say that the first sentence is false. The best answer is (A).

40. The first sentence describes a contentious topic (with the "unpopular" bill), and in the second the governor attempts to explain why that bill was introduced. The best answer is (C).

PART V

Here is a sample response to the essay question:

I agree with the notion that "the people we remember best are the ones who break the rules." Ten people doing what is expected is boring and expected, but that 11th person who is flouting the rules is immediately interesting. I can think of three reasons why I believe this.

In a society based on rules, most of us live within them—either because of a moral desire to do right or a fear of punishment for doing wrong. When we encounter people who have dared to stand in the face of the law, with less regard for the consequences, we often envy their bravery for doing something we cannot. Many times, we can find ourselves living vicariously through another person's exploits that are, statistically, outside the norm.

This is why in movies, for example, the most memorable parts are often of the villains, rather than the heroes. Eliot Ness may have championed the law in a lawless town, but it was Al Capone, his nemesis, whose name so often made the national headlines. When we think of The Silence of the Lambs and The Dark Knight, two movies that earned many favorable reviews and hundreds of millions in revenue, we think less about the heroes than we do about Hannibal Lecter and the Joker. Not coincidentally, the actors who played those roles, Anthony Hopkins and Heath Ledger, earned an Oscar.

On a different note, we also remember people who break the rules because they are the ones mostly likely to come up with something radically new. Bill Gates wasn't deriving value from his studies at Harvard, so he dropped out, formed a software company called Microsoft with his friend Paul Allen, and is now one of the wealthiest men on Earth. Perhaps inspired by this pattern, Mark Zuckerberg did the same thing 30 years later, dropping out of Harvard to start Facebook. And now, he is the world's youngest billionaire.

A society that embraces conformity needs its standouts, those particular people who inspire us to think beyond the accepted and challenge the perception of what is truly possible. Rules mean conformity, and although we need rules to function as a society, we need people to challenge them, bend them, and sometimes break them in order to innovate. Doing so successfully will keep you remembered throughout history, whether you're a criminal or an entrepreneur.

Accuplacer

Appendices

APPENDIX 1: *Grammar Glossary*

Below are several grammar terms this book mentions often, so it's important to know them when you see them referred to in the text. You might know a lot of these terms already, but if you don't, it's not important to spend extra time memorizing them. You won't ever be tested on the terms themselves.

active voice—when the grammatical subject of a sentence performs the action of a sentence (Example: *I threw the ball* is written in the active voice, but *The ball was thrown by me* is in the passive voice.)

adjective—a word used to modify (or describe) a noun or pronoun

adverb—a word usually used to modify a verb and sometimes to modify an adjective or another adverb

antecedent—the noun to which a pronoun refers

appositive—a modifying phrase set in the middle of a sentence and set off by commas

auxiliary verb—a second verb that appears with the main verb of a sentence, often to change its tense (Example: *I go to the store* is in the present tense, but *I **will** go to the store*, which uses the auxiliary verb *will*, is in the future tense.)

article—*A* and *an* are indefinite articles, and *the* is the definite article

clause—a group of words that contains a subject and a verb (see independent clause, dependent clause, subordinate clause, and phrase)

comparative—used when comparing two things (see superlative)

conjugation—the systematic arrangement of all forms of a verb

conjunction—a word used to join other words or groups of words, such as *and*, *but*, and *or*.

dependent clause—a clause that is not a complete sentence and needs to be attached to an independent clause in order for it to be part of a sentence

direct object—a noun that receives the action of a sentence

gerund—the result of adding –*ing* to a verb, thus creating a term used as a noun (Example: *Winning* isn't everything; it's the only thing.)

independent clause—a group of words that expresses a complete thought and can exist alone as a simple sentence

indirect object—the object for which something else is done. (Example: Carl gave the book to his sister. *Book* is the direct object, and *sister* is the indirect object.)

modifier—a descriptive word or phrase

noun—a person, place, thing, quality, or action

participle—a verb form that is used as an adjective (Example: This movie is *exciting*.)

passive voice—when the grammatical subject of a sentence receives the action of a sentence (Example: *I threw the ball* is written in the active voice, but *The ball was thrown by me* is in the passive voice.)

phrase—a group of words that lacks either a noun or verb, and thus is not a clause or a sentence (see also: clause)

preposition—a word that shows the relation between its object and some other word in the sentence (Example: George is perplexed by all the tax regulations. *By* is the preposition, which idiomatically goes with *perplexed*.)

prepositional phrase—a modifying phrase containing a preposition and an object (Example: My dog ran on the beach. *On the beach* describes where the dog ran; *on* is the preposition, and *beach* is the object of that preposition.)

pronoun—a word used in place of a noun for the sake of brevity

proper noun—a noun (such as a name) that designates a particular person, place, or thing; usually begins with a capital letter.

run-on sentence—a sentence in which two independent clauses are linked together without a conjunction or proper punctuation between them (Example: My teacher gives me too much homework, I usually stay up all night doing it.)

split infinitive—an improper verb usage in which the infinitive form is interrupted by another word. (Example: *To* boldly *go* where no one has gone before.)

subject—the noun of a sentence that drives the action

subordinate clause—a clause (also known as a dependent clause) that cannot serve as a sentence by itself and needs to be linked to a main clause

superlative—used when comparing three or more things (see comparative)

verb—the word that denotes the action of a sentence

APPENDIX 2: *Writing Skills and Knowledge*

GRAMMAR (SYNTAX)

Grammar is the study and the formulation of how words relate to one another in a sentence. Consider the non–native attempting to speak English:

"Please…fish…little…cost…good…thank you."

The foreigner doesn't know English grammar. He or she has learned some words but not how to put them together. When the speaker develops his/her language skills, he learns to make connections. He doesn't have to cover his heart with folded hands, drop to his knees, and look longingly with his eyes only. He can say: "*I love you.*" To a native speaker, this sentence seems so "natural," what else could it be? Well, if you were a Roman, the verb would come last, and there would be no separate *I*. In some languages, the three words would be one word alone. In short, there are more than six thousand human languages that we know of, and all of these have different ways of relating words to each other; all have different grammars.

Remarkably, by the time children are three years old they have "learned" the grammar of their native languages. However, like the fish who takes the water it swims in for granted, unless we study our language, we may be unaware that the connections we make are not natural, nor are they given. Rather, we have absorbed a human-made system.

We speak and write our language following rules about how the words and phrases can be strung together. Grammar or syntax is the collection of rules that describe how to connect words, what goes next to what, in which order. To communicate what's inside our heads or hearts to another, we need to know what does, what can, and what words and phases can't go together.

Functions: In addition to rules of relationship, grammar also identifies what the different parts do, or their function. Let's examine the sentence:

Jack looked at Jill lovingly.

Jack is the subject. That is, the function of the word *Jack* is as doer of an action. *Looked* is the action that *Jack* did. We call such action words *verbs. Jill,* unlike Jack, is "the done to." Jill's function is as *object,* not *subject.* Then, take the word *lovingly.* This word functions to describe the verb/action (how did *Jack* look?). *Lovingly* is functioning as an adverb, a part of speech we will soon discuss.

The words and groups of words in any sentence are identified, then, by their function, the way the players in a baseball game are identified. Ted Williams may be the batter at one time, and at another, an outfielder. It depends on what function he is performing. So, too, a word can play various functions depending upon how it relates to other words in a sentence. In the example above, *look* is an action verb, what *Jack* did. However, consider the difference: *The look of love is in your eyes.* In this case, *look* is a noun and subject of the sentence.

EIGHT PARTS OF SPEECH: DESCRIBING THEIR FUNCTIONS

English grammar is built upon the interrelationships of eight functions, or parts of speech: *nouns, pronouns, verbs, adjectives, adverbs, voice, prepositions, and conjunctions.* These are described and studied in this section. We will also identify the grammar and punctuation problems that often occur with parts of speech. Some of these problems are discussed again in other sections.

Nouns

Nouns name people, things, places, animals, items that have shape and form, things we can touch. Things, however, can be less tangible and refer to abstractions such as ideas of freedom, independence, or concepts such as number and shape, or disciplines such as the sciences, the arts. Some nouns name groups of persons or things.

Number: nouns change in number—they can be one (singular), or more than one (plural.) Most nouns show this change in number by adding an *s.* One boat becomes two boats. However, some nouns show number change differently. One woman doesn't become two womans, rather, she becomes two women.

Collective nouns often cause difficulties because of number. They can be confusing because they refer to something made up of more than one.

Jury (of citizens)	flock (of geese)	team (of players)
Band (of musicians)	collection (of coins)	committee (of members)

But grammatically they are treated as singulars, as *its* rather than *theys*. For instance, *"the team played their last game"* is grammatically incorrect and should be *"the team played its last game."*

Types of Nouns

Common Nouns		Proper Nouns	
book, bicycle, cat, ice cream, cars, house, skyscraper		Taylor Lautner, Macy's, General Lee, Justin Bieber, Taylor Swift	
Concrete	**Abstract**		**Collective**
stone, hand, skunk, picture	democracy, free speech, freedom, independence		club, army, squadron, team, committee, group

Noun Case: What do nouns do? First, the subject of a sentence is always a noun, as was *Jack*. But nouns can also be objects, as was *Jill* (the receiver of the verb's action). Or, in their Possessive Case form, nouns are expressing belonging to, or a quality of. Case, then, means the function a noun plays in relationship to other words. There are three cases, and we will see the same when we examine pronouns.

Types of Noun Case

Subjective Case a noun that is the subject	Objective Case a noun that is an object	Possessive Case a noun that owns or belongs to something
The cat chased the mouse. *Cat* is a noun in subjective case.	*The cat chased the mouse.* *Mouse* is a noun in objective case.	*I lost Jack's ticket.* *Jack's* is a noun in possessive case

Note, however, we can rearrange these nouns—depending on what we want to say—changing their function and their case, like moving Ted Williams from the outfield to first base:

> *The mouse escaped from the cat.*

Now, our rodent is the subject, and our *cat* is the object of the preposition *from*. And we mean something different from our first sentence.

Note, too, the noun in the **Possessive Case** indicates ownership by use of apostrophe (') and the letter *s*: *The cat's prey instinct made him constantly hunt for mice.* (whose instinct? *The cat's*). Or, *The girls' dates were all waiting for them outside in the schoolyard.* (Whose dates? *The girls'*.)

Pronouns

Pronouns stand in for a noun and give us ways to substitute for nouns, and thus we can speak with fewer and shorter words and phrases, and with greater variety! Consider what we would face without pronouns:

> *Jimi Hendrix is well-established in the history of music. Hendrix is the King of Rock, and Hendrix's guitar playing is legendary. Jimi Hedrix's death by an overdose made Hendrix an icon of the 1960s. Like Janis Joplin, Jimi Hendrix was the image of overindulgent youth.*

Now, with pronouns:

> *Jimi Hendrix is well-established in the history of music. He is the King of Rock, and his guitar playing is legendary. Jimi Hendrix's death by an overdose made him an icon of the 1960s. Like Janis Joplin, he is the image of overindulgent youth.*

Antecedents: Because a pronoun substitutes for a noun, when one is used, the noun for which it is substituting has to be clear. For example, the pronoun *he* only communicates if we know the noun for which *he* is substituting. An example would be: *He died by assassination.* This sentence without a reference to which the pronoun is referring, makes little sense. However, the following sentence clears up any confusion:

Abraham Lincoln is a symbol as much as he is a former President.
He died by assassination.

Now, the pronoun *he* is comprehensible because we have the antecedent noun for which it is substituting: Abraham Lincoln is *he*.

Antecedent is a term you will see in several important language situations. It means that which comes before. In the case of a pronoun's antecedent, it is the noun to which the pronoun refers. Every pronoun has its "Abraham Lincoln," if it is being used clearly! A clear and consistent relationship between the pronouns and to what or to whom it refers (antecedents) is a major grammar concern called **Pronoun Agreement** (A^2 = Antecedent + Agreement).

Pronoun Types & Cases: In the examples above, we have used different forms of pronouns (*he*, *him*, *I*, and *me*), so let's give these differences a name and description. The most frequently used are the **Personal Pronouns**. But glance at the left column in the table below to view the eight various types of pronouns.

Pronouns: Their Number and Function

Pronoun Types	Singular/Plural	Plural	Function
Personal	*I, me*	*we, us*	Refer to specific persons or things, always to a noun: *The ship is lost. It was last in contact 2 days ago.*
	you, you	*you, you*	
	he, it, she, him, her	*they, them*	
Possessive	*my, mine*	*our, ours*	Indicate possession: *my dog; your cat; his car; our home; their luggage*
	your, yours	*your, yours*	
	his, her, hers, its	*their, theirs*	
Reflexive (intensive)	*myself*	*ourselves*	Emphasize a noun or pronoun: *Myself was shocked.* *You can get your candy yourselves.*
	yourself	*yourselves*	
	him, her, itself	*themselves*	

(continued on next page)

Pronouns: Their Number and Function
(continued from previous page)

Pronoun Types	Singular/Plural	Plural	Function
Demonstrative	*this, that, these, those*		Point to a specific noun, and may also serve as the subject. *That book is controversial.* *That solves the problem.*
Indefinite	*Every, each, everyone, nothing, something, everything no one, nobody, neither, everything, anybody, one* (Number=Singular)		Refer to nonspecific things; mostly function as nouns. But also can work as adjectives. *Something must be done.* *Each day is better than the last.*
	Few, both, many, several (Number=Plural)		Number agreement *Many are called but few are chosen.*
	All, any, more, most, some (can be singular or plural)		*Some of the mail has arrived.* *Some of the letters have arrived.*
Reciprocal	Same as reflexive above		*I gave myself a haircut.*

In addition to the eight types, **pronouns**—like nouns—have three cases. Recall, case refers to function in relations with other words. For instance, the personal pronoun *I* is the **Subjective Case** since its meaning (the doer, the subject) also puts it in a specific relation to another word, a verb:

I gave my ticket away.

I, however, has different meanings and relations with verbs and these differences are expressed by case. Thus, when *I* is not the doer/subject of the verb, it may be the *done to* and object of the verb. When this occurs, the pronoun *I* changes its case to the **Objective Case** and becomes *me*.

John gave me his ticket.

Personal and Relative Pronouns

Pronoun Type	Subjective (Nominative) Case		Objective Case		Possessive Case	
	Singular	**Plural**	**Singular**	**Plural**	**Singular**	**Plural**
Personal Pronoun	I	we	me	us	my, mine	our, ours
	you	you	you	you	your	yours
	he, she,	they	him, her	them	his, hers	their, theirs
	it		it		its	
Relative Pronouns	who	whoever	whom	whomever	whose	whosever

Notice, too, *his*, which expresses belonging, is in the **Possessive Case**. Only two of the eight pronoun types have the case form or aspect. Unlike nouns that show possession by adding an apostrophe *s*, or by changing their ending (e.g., *woman* to *women*) pronouns in the possessive case remain unchanged. The **relative pronouns** bring up an important topic. That is, how we speak is sometimes different from how we write. In speech, we are allowed to be ungrammatical. For instance, many, perhaps most of us, would ask: *Who did you go to the movies with*? But this is not correct. *Who* is not the subject, *you* is the subject. It is the object of the preposition *with*; hence, the question needs the objective case: *Whom did you go to the movies with*? Again, like nouns, pronouns are either singular or plural.

Verbs

Verbs are where the action is! *The cannibals ate their victims.* The **action verb** is *eating*. Another kind of verb doesn't so much describe an action, but rather it connects, and is called a **linking verb**. For example: *Jack seems excited to have gotten that telephone call*. *Seems* is a linking verb; it doesn't describe an action such as eating, or traveling, or snoring. It does connect *Jack* to *excited*, and in making this link, it tells us something about *Jack*.

A third kind of verb is called a **helping verb**. These help another verb—which is the major one—to express a nuance, often a time aspect of the main verb. For instance:

I am going to the movies. Going is the real action, the main verb; *am* is helping by giving *going* the sense of in process. Or, consider this sentence: *I had seen her before she saw me.* Seen is the main verb (act of seeing); *had* is its helping verb. It expresses that the seeing was done earlier, before she saw me. In fact, *to be* and *to have* are the most common, frequently used helping verbs, and they are used primarily to indicate verb tense as you will see below. However, there are other, less common helping verbs, and there are a few more things to be said about active verbs, so let's examine this table below before moving on to verb tenses.

Types of Verbs

Action Verbs Two forms	Linking Verbs Connect the Subject to a complement, usually an adjective or a subject complement (see below)	Helping or Auxiliary Verbs Two forms
Transitive Verb is one that can have an object: *Lincoln gave his famous speech.*	Major linking verbs: *be, feel, become, seem, smell, remain, look, taste, keep, appear, stay, grow, act*	Auxiliary: *to be, to have; to do.* The verbs *to be* and *to have* are so frequently used that you should be familiar with their various forms
Intransitive Verb: does not have an object, usually followed by an adverb: *The Dow fell sharply today.*	*I feel good.* Good is an adjective. *Dr. Jekyll became Mr. Hyde.* Mr. Hyde is the subject complement. *The speaker of the house is Nancy Pelosi.* Nancy Pelosi is the subject complement.	*Modal Auxiliaries* express special meanings such as *obligation, doubt, possibility, can, must, may, should, could, ought to* *He should see a doctor.* *You can travel now.* *She must be on time.*

Grammar Highlight: Action verbs usually are followed by adverbs; but linking verbs are followed by adjectives. Because of how they sound in speech, modals with *have* are often incorrectly written as *of*: *The car must of run out of gas.* Which should read: *The car must have run out of gas.*

Verbs have various forms. Identifying these helps us understand the various ways a verb is used. Right from the start, we need to know how to distinguish between the two forms. Regular verbs follow the same general pattern: add –s on to the verb base to form the 3rd person, singular in present tense. Past tense adds –ed to the base verb. Irregular verbs are stubborn individuals who follow their own patterns (**irregular verbs**). Consequently, since the irregulars are individuals who dance to their own tune, we cannot apply rules to them, but have to learn them as individuals. Irregular verbs change either the 3rd person singular, or the past tense, or both, and some verbs like to be make unique changes in other persons and tenses (see lie, lay, rise below).

Look at the tables above where both *to be* and *to have*, irregular verbs, can be studied and contrasted with regular verbs. All regular verbs follow the same pattern in 3rd person singular and in past tense.

Verb Person

Person	Present Tense Singular (add *s* for 3rd-person singular)		Plural		Past Tense (base+*ed*)	
1st person, singular or plural	I	I act	we	we act	I acted	we acted
2nd person, singular or plural	you	you act	you	you act	you acted	you acted
3rd person, singular or plural	he/she/it	she acts	they	they act	he/she/it acted	they acted
1st person, singular or plural	I want		we want		I wanted	we wanted
2nd person, singular or plural	you want		you want		you wanted	you wanted
3rd person, singular or plural	she wants		they want		they wanted	they wanted

Verb Person: which of the three available is doing the action or linking? Is it the 1st, 2nd, or the 3rd?

Number: as with pronouns, how many? One, or more than one? Singular or plural?

Verb Tense

Present Tense		Past Tense		Past Perfect		Verb Tense
Singular	Plural	Singular	Plural	Singular	Plural	Verb Number
I am you are he/she/ it is	you are we are they are	I was you were he/she/it was	we were you were they were	I have been you have been he, she, it has been	we have been you have been they have been	The underlined verbs identify where agreement problems occur. Note that the verb *to be* uses the verb *to have* as its helping verb to express a past tense.
I have, you have he/she it has	we have you have they have	I had you had he, she, it had	we had you had they had	I have had you have had he, she, it has had	we have had you have had they have had	Note that *to have* uses itself as a helping verb to express the past perfect time.

Regular and Irregular Verbs

Verb form	Regular	Regular	Irregular	Irregular	Irregular	
Base	want	talk	be	have	get	Problems with verb agreement in 3rd person, singular of present tense. Problems with irregular verbs in 3rd person, singular of present tense, and also with past tense
Infinitive	to want	to talk	to be	to have	to get	Infinitive phrase as subject of sentence: *To talk too much is rude.*
Past	wanted	talked	was/ were	had	got	
Past Participle	wanted	talked	been	had	gotten	Past participle–*to be*–forms passive voice *Jesse James was wanted for robbery.*
Present Participle	wanting	talking	being	having	getting	Present in process: *I am talking to her right now.*
Gerund	wanting	talking	being	having	getting	Gerund phrase as subject: *Getting a job has proven to be difficult.*

Verb Tenses: Verbs also change according to the time of their action or linking. These time changes are called **tenses**. Consider how tense adds to our ability to communicate with one another. Imagine, for instance, arriving at someone's house who, being a generous host, offers you lunch. We take for granted that it's a simple matter to decline without offense by explaining: *No, thank you, I ate lunch but an hour ago.* If we had no past tense, we would be forced to act out and hope to be understood, perhaps by: "I eat..." and then indicating past by gesturing behind our shoulder with our hand.

In writing, we dramatically alter the meaning of what we say by our use of tense:

> *I was studying when the lights went out and threw the dorm into darkness for the rest of the evening.*

> *I had already studied when the lights went out and threw the dorm into darkness for the rest of the evening.*

Present Tense: actions occurring now, actions occurring regularly, or general truths:

> *I see you sitting there; every day.*

> *I speak to the homeless man.*

> *Love is stronger than hate.*

Past Tense: Actions that happened before now and are over and done with:

> *I ate dinner an hour ago.*

Future Tense: Action that will happen in the future:

> *I will eat dinner within the hour.*

Finally, there are a few verbs that give people trouble such as the differences between the verbs *to lay* and *to lie*, or those between *raise* and *rise*.

Irregular Verbs–*To Lay*, *To Lie* or *To Rise*

Infinitive	Present Participle	Present Tense	Past Tense	Past Participle
To lie—recline, be prostrate	lying	lie: *he lies in bed*	lay	lain
To lay—to place	laying	lay	laid	laid
To rise	rising	rise	rose	risen
To raise	raising	raise	raise	raised
To lie—express a falsehood	lying	lie	lied	lied

Subject Verb Agreement (agr): Speaking trains native speakers to follow this rule quite 'naturally'; however, there are some grammatical structures that give many writers problems. First, let's look at the typical sentence and how the law of agreement works:

Yesterday the children ate their lunches at their desks.

The verb must agree with the subject's person and number. The subject is *children*; its number is plural and its person is the 3rd (see chart above). Now it's true that the writer also had to know the correct past form of the verb *eat* which is *ate* and not *eated*, and also the correct tense.

Most agreement problems have to do with number, which means determining if the subject is singular or plural. Indeed, verb agreement with subject is very similar to pronoun agreement with antecedents, and the chart below will help this.

Verb Agreement

Problem or Issue	Verb must agree with number of subject	Pronoun must agree with number of antecedent
Compound subject: two subjects connected by *and* (N=P)	*Susan B. Anthony and Elizabeth Cady Stanton were extraordinary women; they were geniuses.*	*Susan B. Anthony and Elizabeth Cady Stanton were extraordinary women; they were geniuses.*
Compound Subject: one entity despite appearing to be two subjects (N=S)	*Ben & Jerry's makes the best ice cream.*	*Do you like Ben & Jerry's? It's my favorite!*
Subject separated from verb can confuse	*The winner amongst all the contestants goes to the Caribbean.* Or, *The winners of the race go to the Caribbean.*	*The winner amongst all the contestants goes to the Caribbean. He or she will be happy.* *The winners of the race go to the Caribbean. They will be happy.*

(continued on next page)

Verb Agreement
(continued from previous page)

Problem or Issue	Verb must agree with number of subject	Pronoun must agree with number of antecedent
Indefinite Pronoun	*Each of the contestants gets a new car.* Generally Singular	*Each of the contestants gets a new car. He or she will select a model.*
Correlative Conjunctions: Neither...nor Either... or	Verb agrees with number of the subject closest to it (or the 2nd subject) *Neither the stockholders nor the CEO seems concerned about the sudden dip in profits.*	Pronoun agrees with the antecedent closest to it. *Neither the stockholders nor the CEO seems concerned about the sudden dip in the profits of his company.*
Collective Nouns (N=S) Generally Singular	*The committee announces the much awaited decision today.* *Economics is a tough subject as is statistics.* *Measles/mumps keeps you in bed.*	*The committee announces its much awaited decision today.* *Economics gets its bad reputation from its many false predictions.*
Postponed subject: subject follows the verb Verb agrees with subject (not complement)	*At the end of the corridor is a small door.* *The real power is the men behind the scenes.*	*At the end of the corridor is a small door, it's black and tan. The real power is the men behind the scenes, hidden though it is, it's what really makes things happen*
Who, which, that can confuse	*Lucinda is the one who rescued the bird.* *The boys want to be on the team that scores highest.*	
Gerund phrase: a gerund with object Gerund phrases take singular form	*Following speeding cars is a dangerous thing to do.*	*Following speeding cars is dangerous. Doing it is a foolish thing to do.*

Voice: Active and Passive

English strongly prefers that the subject come first, followed by the verb, then by the object or recipient of the actions, or, if a linking verb, by a subject complement or an adjective.

> *The batter hit→→the ball hard.*

> *The Academy of Film Arts gave→→Julia Roberts an award.*

This pattern with the subject going toward (with the verb) the object (formula, S+V+O) is the *Active Voice*.

However, writers sometimes (correctly, often incorrectly) use the *Passive Voice*. This reverses the formula, O+V+S, making a sentence with the object of the verb first, then the verb, and finally, the subject.

> *The ball was hit hard by the ←batter.*

The action is turned around, the subject, *batter*, fades and the focus is on the object, the *ball*. In short, the passive voice puts the object in the limelight, and it weakens both the act (the verb action) and the subject (the doer). By contrast, then, the active voice highlights the subject and emphasizes that she/he is the doer. So, when is it correct to use the passive voice? Answer: when the object is more important than the subject. Consider:

> *Natalie Portman was awarded an Oscar for her performance in* The Black Swan.

Or in the active voice:

> *The committee awarded Natalie Portman an Oscar.*

The first sentence is preferred because the fact that Portman won the Oscar is more important than the committee that did the awarding. Now let's examine the structure of that passive voice: *Natalie Portman* is the object, *was rewarded*, the verb, and the subject has so faded from importance that it isn't even in the sentence!

Was rewarded also shows us the formula for a passive voice verb = to be + past participle.

> *The* Mona Lisa *is considered a Renaissance masterpiece by most art critics.*

Is (to be) *considered* is the past participle of *consider*. In this case the doer is nowhere to be seen. A much stronger, active sentence is:

> *Art critics consider the* Mona Lisa *a masterpiece.*

Here's another case: *This is to inform you that your application has been rejected.* By who? As a rule, the active voice is the most effective, and it's always more concise and less wordy.

While in a few instances, using the passive voice is fine, and, more rarely still, preferred, in the vast majority of instances, the passive voice is discouraged for two good reasons: the passive voice is weaker because the subject as actor is backstage—if present at all, in the rear rather than up-front. Thus, "the action" is muted and diluted. The passive voice is more wordy—always. Count the words in the two sentences above. Count them in the two following sentences:

> Active: *The instructor discussed the requirements and the time schedule for this semester's class.*

> Passive Voice: *The requirements and the time schedule for this semester's course were discussed by the teacher.*

Adjectives and Adverbs

Adjectives are words that describe nouns or pronouns. We use adjectives a lot in speech and writing; many common ones pepper our conversations. For example: *a good day*; *a soft sound*; *a yellow car*.

Adverbs have more possible roles than the adjective. Adverbs can describe verbs (*he spoke slowly*); they can describe adjectives (*His face had a sickly yellow look. She is very sad.*); they can describe adverbs like *themselves*; they can describe infinitives (*he was urged to go quickly.*)

Adverbs often answer the question *how*? How did he go? *Quickly*.

Adverbs often end in *–ly*: *quickly, smoothly, sleepily, coldly*

Those adverbs that don't end in *–ly* are often those that refer to time and frequency:

today, yesterday, often tomorrow, soon, never, always, never, sometimes

> **Grammar Highlight:** Remembering that adjectives modify nouns, and that, contrarily, adverbs modify verbs, adjectives, or another adverb will help you to identify what a prepositional phrase is doing in a sentence.

Prepositions

Your teachers may have advised: "Never end a sentence with a preposition!" But what's a preposition? We use them very frequently (look at the list below), but defining them clearly is difficult. Prepositions, for instance, are words that connect a noun to other parts of its sentence. Or, prepositions are words that express space (*on the table*), time (*at the appointed hour*), and direction (*towards the North Pole*). There are two kinds of prepositions—simple, one-word prepositions, and group prepositions.

It's easier to get a handle on the simple, one-word prepositions by identifying them in the prepositional phrase (where they most often are to be found, except when they end a sentence by themselves!). You will find the preposition before a noun or a pronoun, and it will almost always be working as an adjective or an adverb, modifying a part of the sentence of which it is itself a part. Here are the most common:

above, behind, except, off, toward

above, below, for, on, under

across, beneath, from, onto, underneath

after, beside, in, out, until

against, between, inside, outside, up

along, beyond, into, over, upon

among, by, like, through, with

around, despite, near, throughout, within

at, during, of, to, without

Group prepositions are made up of more than one word:

in addition to	in place of
next to	in front of
as well as	along with
according to	due to
in conjunction with	because of

Infinitives: The word *to* is one of the most used prepositions. When you find it, you are fairly sure that it is the first word in a prepositional phrase. However, another important construction using the word *to* is the **verb infinitive**, the base of a verb preceded by *to*. Infinitives: *to go*; *to see*; *to believe*; *to investigate*. All verbs have this simple infinitive form.

In a sentence, the infinitive can be a noun, both subject:

> *To read is heaven on earth to Julia.*

or an object,

> *Julia likes to read.*

An infinitive can be the subjects complement:

> *It is the responsibility of all expert detectives to investigate a crime for as long as it takes.*

Conjunctions

Conjunctions come in four basic varieties. They work to join parts of sentence, to join together words, or phrases, or clauses, or even sentences. *And* is probably the most used conjunction––observe how frequently we use it to join words: *apples and oranges; work and play; sing and dance; toys and hobbies; Bill and Sally.*

And is also one of a group of **coordinating conjunctions**: for, and, nor, but, or, yet, so, otherwise know as **FANBOYS**. We'll use that term throughout the appendix when we refer to these coordinating conjunctions. These FANBOYS help create compound sentences, and when they serve this role, a comma comes before their use.

Correlative conjunctives: Remember these by their "relatives." These are twins such as *neither/nor, either/or, not/only, but/also, both/and.*

Subordinating conjunctions are

after	if	so that
although	in case	than
as if	in that	though
as though	insofar as	unless
because	no matter	how until
before	now that	when, whenever
even if	once	where, wherever
even though	provided that	whether
how	since	while

Conjunctive adverbs—make brain connection with semi-colons and commas.

however, then	*She went to the film; however, I didn't go.*
therefore, hence	*It rained hard and fast; therefore, we stayed home.*
also, consequently	*The book focused on a popular topic; also, its central character was controversial.*

| thus, nevertheless | *The importer pays the taxes, then sells the articles at an inflated price; thus it is the consumer who ultimately pays.* |

Interjections: These are odd-balls in that they almost contradict our definition of a part of speech as defined by its function to other words. This is because they do not really function in relationship, but rather stand outside the grammatical connections. An interjection is strong expression, a powerful emotion, a cry from the soul that sometimes is barely a word:

> *O Heavenly Father, help us in this time of hardship!*

> *Oh, she cried!*

> *Yikes!*

> *Help!*

When we spill over in exasperation, we are likely to express ourselves in interjection:

> *oh hell; fine; drop dead; scram*

Articles: These are so numerous in speech and writing that we want to give them a special focus even though they are not one of the eight parts of speech. *A, an, the*: Meet the articles—they always come before a noun. General vs. specific noun: *A* or *a* functions to identify a noun referring to something in general: *a book; a door; a cat. The* functions to identify or point to a specific: *the book, the cat, the door.* Spelling articles: *a* is used when the noun it identifies starts with a consonant: *a book, a door, a cat. An* is used when the noun starts with a vowel: *an elf, an apple, an ice cream cone, an ox, an ulcer.*

THE SENTENCE

The previous section reacquainted you with grammar or syntax: the laws of relationships and the function of the components of English, the eight parts of speech. This section focuses on the sentence: what it is (definition); what it does (function); what it's made of (structure and criteria); its four forms (meanings), its four types (variations in structure); and the punctuation that sentences use to fulfill their function: to express a thought! In this section we will also identify the major grammatical and punctuation problems related to sentence structure.

What defines a sentence? Basically it is a complete thought—that is, it's a grammatical unit that is composed of one or more clauses. Clauses are units of words that form a complete thought. The function of a sentence is to express an idea, a fact, or a desire.

Examples: *I want an ice cream.*
We left the restaurant at midnight.

Sentence Function

Type	Example	Grammar Rules
Declaratory Sentence States, expresses a point <u>Thesis statement</u> is a declaratory sentence.	*Logan, the adorable pit–bull, licked his owner's face.*	All sentences begin with a capital; declaratory sentences end with a period.
Interrogatory Sentence Asks a question	*Did Logan lick her face?*	Begins with a capital; interrogatory sentences end with question marks.
Imperative Sentence Gives an order or a direction to another	*Lick her face and jump all over her.*	Begins with a capital; ends usually with a period, but sometimes with an exclamation point. The subject is often hidden, or "understood." The subject is whoever is being given the direction (Logan, you) *lick her face, jump all over her–– right now!*
Exclamatory Sentence Expresses emotion!	*What a handsome dog!*	Begins with a capital; often exclamatory sentences end with exclamation points. Writers are urged to use such sentences and punctuation only rarely. Overuse takes away their expressive power.

As we speak, the listener knows when our thought is complete by our inflection, by the tone of our voice, or by our body language. In writing, two signals "tell" the reader: "Mission accomplished!" The capital marks the start, the ending punctuation (period, question mark; exclamation point) in effect, says, "I'm done." When we incorrectly give the signal telling the reader that we are finished, but it isn't a complete thought—we cause confusion. This signal malfunction creates a *sentence fragment*. To qualify as a sentence, and earn its punctuation marks, a group of words must meet three criteria:

1. it must have a subject.

2. it must have a verb (and often has a verb <u>predicate</u>, verb + other words).

3. It must be a complete thought (this is the criteria that a fragment does not meet!).

Sentence Fragments

Fragment	Analysis	Corrective Sentence	Structure
Seeing you in the supermarket.	No subject (actually no verb either as you will see in the section on phrases). *Seeing* is a gerund.	*I saw you in the supermarket.*	Subject (I) verb (saw) predicate (you in the supermarket)
In the produce section at the back of the store.	No subject. No verb. Two prepositional phrases	*I saw you in the produce section at the back of the store.*	Subject (I) verb (saw) predicate (you in the produce section at the back of the store)
Since it rained last night.	Subject (it) Verb predicate (rained last night.) Complete thought? No!	*Since it rained last night, we canceled our stargazing appointment.*	The additional words complete the thought and meet the criteria Subject (we) verb (canceled) predicate (our stargazing appointment)

Sentence Patterns

English sentences tend to fall into patterns, and be represented as formulas. The following are the **major ones**.

Pattern 1

Formula	Subject (noun or pronoun)	Intransitive Verb (no object)
S+V	The population	has tripled.

Pattern 2

Formula	Subject	Transitive verb	Object
S+V+O	The thunder	awakened	the children.

Pattern 3

Formula	Subject	Linking Verb	Complement
S+V+C	The effects of climate change	are	catastrophic.
	The children	must be	tired.
	The leader	is	General Mottard.

Pattern 4

Formula	Subject	Transitive verb	Indirect object	Direct Object
S+V+IO+DO	The Professor	gave	Julie	a good grade.

Pattern 5

Formula	Subject	Transitive Verb	Direct Object	Object Complement
S+V+DO+OC	The critics	proclaimed	the film	a triumph.

Four Sentence Types

Structure	Grammar & Punctuation	Meaning	Style
Simple: One independent clause: Subject (S) + Verb/predicate (V)	Do not use commas to separate S from V	One idea, point, statement, or question is expressed	Too many create choppiness and disconnection amongst the ideas/points
Compound: Two or more independent clauses that are connected to form one sentence	Two connectors only: 1. FANBOYS preceded by comma 2. Semi-colon **Not** by comma (cs)! Comma after conjunctive adverbs: *therefore, however, thus, hence*, etc. $\Longrightarrow$	Each of the independent clauses is an idea/point and connecting them expresses that they are of equal value. Points that are **not** related and/or are not of equal value should not be compound sentences. *The storm raged; therefore, school was canceled.* *Logan is a pit-bull mix; however, contrary to myths, he is a gentle fellow.*	Helps reader see connection between ideas; fosters the feeling of "flow" Semi-colon is a powerful link with dramatic meaning In a compound sentence, linked with a semi-colon, followed by a conjunctive adverb, place comma after the adverb:

(continued on next page)

Four Sentence Types
(continued from previous page)

Structure	Grammar & Punctuation	Meaning	Style
Complex: one independent clause plus one or more dependent clauses	Dependent clauses function as modifiers: 1. Adjective clauses 2. Adverb clauses 3. Noun Clauses <u>Subordinate clauses</u> connect a related but less important idea to the main idea expressed in the independent clause. Commas when clause begins sentence Commas only for <u>nonrestrictive</u> clauses	The point in the independent clause is in some way <u>modified</u> or <u>qualified</u>, rather than equivalence as in compound *If you go to the movies, we will meet you there. Keena, <u>who mothered our five pups</u>, won the Westminster," Most Adorable Dog" trophy. The boy <u>who threw the rock</u> will be expelled.*	Help reader make accurate connection between ideas Readers need a break from too many in a row
Compound–Complex: two or more independent clauses and one or more dependent clauses	1+ 2 above	Number of idea or points connected is increased	Readers **need** a break from too many in a row

Simple Sentence: "Simple," in this case, doesn't mean short, nor does it mean that it is non-complex. Rather, it refers to its structure—to what its parts are. A simple sentence can be very long, but it will have only one **independent clause**.

Independent Clause: is a synonym for sentence. Another way of saying this: A sentence is an independent clause, or it is made up of more than one independent clause. Whenever you come across the phrase *independent clause*, think—it meets the three criteria for a sentence. We'll examine clauses in the paragraphs below. Here is a short simple sentence.

> *Proust and Gide are the best known French writers of the 20th century.*

Here's another a little longer.

> *Both Proust and Gide wrote for a 20th century audience and yet retained their relevance for readers of the 21st century.*

And longer still:

> *In the end, against our wishes, in opposition to all advice, <u>our son, John, and the neighbor's daughter, Janice, dropped</u> out of school, <u>left</u> all their friends and family, and <u>embarked</u> on a trip across country despite the poor weather and the high cost of fuel.*

Note: the underlined sections identify the skeleton of the one independent clause: compound subject and compound verb (three of them). The rest of the sentence is primarily prepositional phrases.

Compound Sentence: is one that has more than one independent clause, and no dependent clauses.

Examples:

> <u>*The children baked three pies*</u>, *and* <u>*they took all of them to the patients*</u>.
>
> <u>*Barack Obama began the presidential campaign of 2008 behind Hillary Clinton*</u>, *but* <u>*he still managed to win*</u>.

Look closely at each of the underlined sections. Think back on the sentence pattern. Identify how each has a subject + verb predicate, and each is a complete thought. Therefore, each of them <u>could be</u> a separate sentence. As the examples demonstrate, *compound sentences* connect independent clauses into one sentence, rather than allowing them to stand alone. They do this in **two** ways **only**:

1. With a *coordinating conjunction* (FANBOYS = *for, and, nor, but, or, yet, so*), and, as the two sentences illustrate, a *comma before* the coordinating conjunction.

2. *Compound sentences* are also linked with semi-colons.

    The victor is the quickest; Jane Levin's the sure winner! Or:

    Wealth is often coarse; poverty is frequently refined.

> **Grammar Highlight:** a common comma error stems from not differentiating between the *and* connecting two independent clauses (**requiring a comma**) from the *and, or, but,* that is connecting a compound verb (**no comma**):
>
> *John scored well below his average level of performance, but he still passed the test.* (Compound Sentence)
>
> *John scored well below his average level of performance but still passed the test.* (Simple sentence with one subject, John, and a compound verb: scored/passed)

When do you choose a FANBOYS connection, or the semi-colon? The semi-colon is often used to pull the two independent clauses closer together for dramatic effect. Consider the dramatic difference between these two sentences:

> *John studied hard, but he still failed.*
>
> *John studied hard; he still failed.*

Or imagine how much less dramatic with a FANBOYS:

> *He came; he saw; he conquered.*

> **Grammar Note:** Linking **two independent clauses** is generally the **only** correct use of a semi-colon in the middle of a sentence. When you see a semi-colon, check on each side for a sentence that could stand alone. Other, less frequent semi-colon use is to separate items in series, when the items have internal punctuation.

The next sentence type is the ***complex sentence***. They contain one independent clause plus one or more dependent clauses (IC+DC, or IC+DC+DC). Let's look at a complex sentence with more than one dependent clause:

> <u>When the ship comes in</u>, he will get a handsome paycheck <u>even though he never lifted a hand in actually delivering the goods to port</u>.

This combination of one or more dependent clauses in a sentence with an independent clause forms a ***complex sentence***. Let's examine how dependent clauses in a complex sentence function:

> *Linguists have discovered at least three ancient languages.*

This is a **simple sentence: one independent clause**. However, we change it to a ***complex sentence*** by adding a dependent clause:

> *Linguists have discovered at least three ancient languages <u>that may be the origin of all others</u>.*

Complex–compound sentences are made of at least one dependent clause (making it complex) and two or more independent clauses (making it compound):

> **Because Gene has always been a big eater**, <u>no one was surprised at his obesity</u>, and <u>his congestive heart diagnosis also came as no surprise</u>.

The underlining identifies the two independent clauses. The phrase in bold is the dependent clause. It's <u>not</u> the length of the sentence but its <u>structure</u> that makes it a **compound-complex sentence**–at least two independent clauses plus at least one dependent clause (2 IC+DC). Here's another example:

> ***Since Susan B. Anthony was such a staunch proponent of justice in the long struggle for women's suffrage***, <u>the U.S. Postal Service finally, and justly, issued a stamp in her honor; we can only hope</u> **that such recognition will follow quickly for Elizabeth Cady Stanton; after** all, <u>Stanton and Anthony were indivisible beings</u>, in a partnership **that transcended space.**

The underlining identifies the three independent clauses; the bold identifies the three dependent clauses that make up this **compound-complex sentence**. Note that the dependent clause adds more information to the complete thought of the independent clause. This addition of more information is called *modifying*.

> *Since Susan B. Anthony was such a staunch proponent of justice in the long struggle for women's suffrage*, the U.S. Postal Service finally, and justly, issued a stamp in her honor.

Clauses

Let's begin our discussion of clauses by examining the simple sentences from the vantage of clause language:

> *Proust and Gide*(**A**) *wrote*(**B**) *for a 20ᵗʰ century audience and yet retained*(**C**) *their relevance for readers of the 21st century.*

> *Proust and Gide* (**A**) *are the subjects, a* **compound subject** *because it has more than one actor.*

(**B**) and (**C**) are the clause's **compound verb**. Both *wrote* and *retained* belong to the **subject**, *Proust and Gide*. Take away all the other words, and you see the skeleton pattern (S+V) clearly: *Proust and Gide wrote and retained.*

Grammar Highlight: Comma errors often occur in sentences with **compound verbs**. The writer mistakenly places a comma before the *and*, thus separating the verbs that must, for clarity, remain together. Consider this sentence:

Dublin, the awesome pit-bull who lives down the street, habitually barks at, and chases cars.

The sentence reads much smoother if we take out the comma after *barks at*.

Dublin, the awesome pit-bull who lives down the street, habitually barks at and chases cars.

Let's examine a sentence with a ***simple subject*** (one) and a ***simple verb*** (only one):

> ***In the afternoon, after our long hike,*** we <u>took a very long nap</u>.

We is the subject; the underlined words are the verb predicate (S+VP). It is a complete thought. This is a simple sentence. The words indicated in **bold** are two prepositional phrases.

Summary: An ***independent clause*** is a group of words that has a subject, a verb, and is a complete thought. Since it meets all the criteria of a sentence, it can be one! It's independent, then, because it is capable of standing alone as a sentence—with a capital and an ending punctuation. However, as in **compound sentences**, independent clauses are sometimes connected, so that there are two, or three, or even, four, or five of them in one compound sentence.

Dependent Clause as the name suggests needs "someone to lean on" because even though it has a <u>subject</u> and a <u>verb</u>, it does not meet the 3rd criterion of a sentence: it is not a complete thought!

> *Whenever a new discovery is made.* (S=*discovery*, V= *is made.*)

But, ***what*** happens when a discovery is made?

> *If we go to church.* (S=*we*, V=*go*)

Yes? ***What*** if we go to church?

In fact, in their current formation (incorrectly telling the reader they are sentences with the capitals and periods), they are ***sentence fragments***. However, we can use them if we complete the thought:

> *Whenever a new scientific discovery is made, <u>society</u> inevitably <u>benefits</u>.*

Look at the description of dependent clauses below to see the different ways that dependent clauses add information to, or modify their independent partners in a complex sentence.

How Clauses Modify

Clause Type	Example	Typical Words	Grammar
Adjective Clause: modifies noun or pronoun	*The idea that girls can't do math discourages female achievement.* *He who is without fault should cast the first stone.*	**Relative pronouns**: *that, which, who, whom, whose, whoever*	*That* is often 'understood': The values (that) I most appreciate.
Adverb Clause: modifies verb, adjective, or another adverb	*Since the women's movement of the 60s and 70s, many women are keeping their maiden names.* *Names are powerful because they bestow existence.*	**Subordinating conjunctions**: *since, when, although, if, before, in order that, while, after* $\Longrightarrow$	When subordinate clauses begin a sentence, always follow them with a comma. When they come at the end, a comma is often not used.
Noun Clause: does all a single noun does: • Subject • Object	*What we force ourselves to forget often returns through an underground leak.* *I cannot forgive that you wished me harm.*	How, who, which, who, whomever, whether, whose, why, what whatever, where, that	Do not use comma after a noun clause subject.

Restrictive and Non-Restrictive Clauses, Misplaced Modifiers, and Parallelism

Identifying the grammar problems of these three issues depends greatly on the ability to identify the clauses we have just studied. These three are also very frequent problem areas for students, so understanding them is especially important.

Identifying the difference between restrictive and non–restrictive clauses will also tell you when to use **that** and **which**. **Restrictive clauses** are necessary to the sentence's meaning therefore use **that**. **Non–restrictive clauses** are not necessary to the main meaning so you would use **which** plus **commas**. Here is a **complex** sentence with **restrictive clause** underlined:

The poet <u>who served as England's Laureate throughout Victoria's reign</u> was none other than Alfred, Lord Tennyson.

Why is that clause necessary to the meaning? Because if we did not have this information, we wouldn't know which poet is being discussed. Here's another example of a restrictive clause in a complex sentence:

The buildings <u>that are scheduled for demolition</u> are marked with red paint.

Try taking that restrictive clause out. Note that without the information in the **restrictive clause**, one cannot identify why the buildings are painted red and, therefore, cannot identify which buildings need to be removed.

Non-restrictive clauses add some information too, but their information is not vital to the main point of the independent clause in which they are embedded:

John Wilkes Booth, <u>who was an actor</u>, shot Lincoln in a theatre in front of the players and the audience.

The commas tell the reader: *here's a bit of interesting information*. But knowing that Booth was an actor is not necessary to the main meaning—that he shot Lincoln in full view of the audience and actors. Here's another to reinforce that **which** is preferred over **that** in a non–restrictive clause:

<u>Lost</u>, the television series, which was created five years ago, won three prizes at last night's award ceremonies.

In the examples below, *which* is selected to head the clause in the second sentence because the clause gives the reader additional information. Unlike the first sentence, the information does not alter the meaning, nor is the correct understanding of the sentence dependent upon it.

The revolution that dramatically changed the form of Russian society began in 1905 with a bread strike.

The Russian revolution, which to this day has worldwide reverberations, began in 1905 and dramatically changed Russian society.

Who, *whom*, *whoever*, *whoever* are often confusing to writers. The key to using them correctly is **pronoun case**. Review the pronoun case chart previously displayed in the chapter. *Who* and *whoever* are **subject case** and *whomever* and *whom* are **object case**. Remember, too, that in speaking we commonly are ungrammatical. It's ok in speaking, but not in writing!

> *Who killed Abraham Lincoln and altered American history?*

Ask yourself what is the subject of "killed and altered"? It is *who* and thus the choice is correct.

> *To whom is much given and thus is much expected?*

In this case the presence of the preposition, *to*, would require the objective *whom*. In addition, *to whom* is the indirect object of the verb *given*.

> *The law decreed that whoever violated the letter would be exiled forever.*
> (Who violated the law?)

> *The book would belong to whomever won the spelling bee.*

Phrases

Phrases look different from clauses—they do **not** have both a subject and verb. And, they do **not** determine sentence type as do the presence of independent and dependent clauses.

Major Types of Phrases

1. Verbal phrases (those made with various verb parts).

2. Prepositional phrases

3. Appositive phrases

Verbal Phrase. A ***verbal phrase*** uses a form of verb but the new form <u>doesn't</u> function like a verb (to show action, to help, or to link). Instead, depending on the type, they function as nouns, adjectives, or adverbs.

Verbal Phrases

Types of Verb Phrase	Structure	Function	Example	Grammar
Gerund	Verb base *–ing* *singing*	Noun, and like a noun, a gerund can be subject or object	*Beautifully pitched <u>singing</u> is her trademark.* *She was applauded for her <u>singing</u>.*	Almost always require singular verb or pronoun form.
Infinitive Phrase	to a verb base *to sing*	Functions as a noun, an adjective, or an adverb	*To sit for hours is boring.* *She has many books <u>to read.</u>* *They design casinos <u>to make</u> people want <u>to spend</u> money.*	adjective modifying the noun, *books to make* modifies verb, *design;* to spend is noun object of *want*
Participial Phrases	present participle/ or past participle: *sleeping* *frightened*	adjectives, often right after the noun	*The Judge, <u>looking stern</u>, emphatically delivered the death sentence.* *The dogs, frightened by the sirens, hid under the bed.* *Frightened by the sirens, the dogs hid under the bed.*	**Commas** often around them when in the middle of a sentence, or after them when they come before an independent clause
Absolute Phrase	A noun or pronoun, or participle or any modifiers that go with these	Modifies the whole remainder of the sentence	*<u>His voice rising to a shriek</u>, the teacher scared the students with his sharp criticism.* *The tower, <u>its bells ringing loudly</u>, announced the ceremony's start.* *The squad used the cover of night to infiltrate the town, <u>surrounding and containing everyone residing there</u>.*	Note that unlike the participial phrase above, this one has a subject (*his voice*). **Commas** follow an absolute phrase that comes at the beginning, surround one the comes in the middle, and precede one that comes at the end of a sentence.

Prepositional Phrases begin with a ***preposition*** and they end with a ***noun***. In the sentence below the underlined words are all prepositional phrases. But note that *to buy* is an infinitive—*to* with the verb *buy*.

> All <u>of the children</u> ran <u>to the corner store</u> to buy candy <u>for the movies</u>.

Prepositional phrases are always working as either an ***adjective*** or an ***adverb***. Prepositional phrases that are functioning as adjectives are almost always right after the noun or pronoun they modify. Ask the question after *all* (indefinite pronoun) *what*? Or after *candy* (a noun), *which candy*? The candy *for the movies* answers the question. On the other hand, *to the corner store* modifies the verb *ran*; its functions, then, as an adverb, answering the adverb question, *Where did they run*?

> **Grammar Highlight:** Remember that adjectives modify nouns, and that, contrarily, adverbs modify verbs, adjectives, or other adverbs. They will help you to identify what a prepositional phrase is doing in a sentence.

Appositive Phrases are nouns that *describe* another noun or pronoun.

> *Abraham Lincoln, the 16th President of the U.S., is considered by many the greatest of our leaders.*

What makes this a phrase? First, it's more than one word; second, the main definition or defining word is the ***noun***, *President*. Appositive phrases nearly always require commas. If one comes in the middle, then commas are placed around the phrase.

> *American track-and-field athlete Jesse Owens, <u>the winner of four Gold Medals at the 1936 Olympic Games</u>, was a black man.*

If one comes at the beginning of a sentence, then the comma follows.

> <u>*A big thief without a doubt*</u>*, Madoff deserves life in prison.*

Parallelism (//)

Language shares much with music, beginning, of course, with its basic reliance upon sounds and being heard. **Parallelism** requires that elements in a sentence that are <u>in series</u> or that are being <u>compared or contrasted</u> be expressed in the same grammatical and syntactical form.

Let's look at parallelism <u>in series</u> construction: *it's only a <u>hop</u>, <u>skip</u>, and <u>jump</u> away*. All three items are nouns, and this makes the sentence flow. Contrast the effect of violating parallelism: *it's only a <u>hop</u>, <u>skip</u>, and <u>jumping</u> away*. The switch from a simple noun to a gerund phrase sounds awkward and it confuses the meaning. Consider, again, the difference:

> *Government of the people, by the people, for the people.*

Perfect parallelism such as this is a masterful rhetorical style. Note that each item in the series is a prepositional phrase. In contrast to:

> *Government of the people, by the people, and with the needs of the people foremost.*

Changing the 3rd item of the series from one prepositional phrase to two alters the rhythm and flow of the phrase, significantly damaging its impact. Sentences that violate parallelism disturb the reader like an off-key note disturbs a listener; both jolt and distract. The smooth flow of meaning is stopped until the reader can remove the blockage.

Parallelism in Sentences

Structures	Non Parallel	Parallel
Items in series	*Hobbits also love adventures, traveling, and dream of becoming heroes with swords.*	*Hobbits love adventure, traveling, and dreams of heroism.*
Comparisons Comparisons such as those made with **correlative conjunctions** that commonly come in pairs: *either…or; not only…but also; whether… or.*	*The Hobbits were not only fearless warriors but also their friendship was something you could rely upon.* *He is neither a scoundrel nor does he aspire to dominate others.*	*The Hobbits were not only fearless warriors but they were also loyal friends.* *He is neither a scoundrel nor a tyrant.*
Lists and outlines	*I will do three things to improve my listening skills:* *Avoid interrupting* *Eliminate noise* *Eye-contact*	*I will do three things to improve my listening skills:* *Avoid interrupting* *Eliminate noise* *Maintain eye-contact*

Misplaced and Dangling Modifiers

Modifiers are words or phrases that describe, identify, and specify another part of a sentence. We have examined adjectives, adverbs, adjective clauses, and adverb clauses—how they are used, how they are punctuated. How they are located in a sentence is another major concern. As the term indicates, a **Misplaced Modifier (mm)** is one not correctly positioned in its sentence. These are often the cause of unintended humor–and lack of clear meaning!

I saw the sick skunk <u>driving down the street</u>.

He wore a red beret on his head, which was much too small.

The underlined modifying phrase/clauses are placed next to the wrong nouns. The sentences need to be revised to place them next to the nouns they do modify:

> *Driving down the street, I saw the sick skunk.*

> *He wore a red beret, which was much too small, on his head.*

Dangling Modifiers (dm), too, are often sources of humor and twisted meaning:

> *<u>Although exhausted and demoralized</u>, the coach kept insisting on another lap.*

> *<u>Hanging by one toe from the rope 300 feet above</u>, the performance was the most exciting of the circus.*

The underlined modifiers are problematic because they refer to a subject who is either absent from the sentence or whose identity is unclear. In the above, the track team is missing as is the high rope performer. Revision is required:

> *Although the track team was exhausted and demoralized, the coach insisted on another lap.*

> *Hanging by one toe from the rope 300 feet above, the high rope expert gave the most exciting performance of the circus.*

Here's one in which the subject of the modifier is present but unclear:

> *<u>With only a 3.0 GPA</u>, Rutgers's graduate school nonetheless accepted Sarah.*

As it is, Rutgers has a 3.0 GPA requirement. Revision:

> *Sarah, with only a 3.0 GPA, was accepted by Rutgers.*

Squinting Modifiers occur when a modifier is placed between two words, either one of which could be its anchor. This confuses:

> *We were certain <u>at noon</u> our trip was canceled.*

Does the writer mean: *At noon, we were certain our tip was canceled, or that our trip was canceled at noon?*

Placement of adverbs: *Only, just, merely*

Proper placement of these adverbs can determine and alter the **meaning** of a sentence.

For instance, consider the different meanings of:

> *I eat <u>only</u> one dessert per day.*
>
> *I <u>only</u> eat one dessert per day.*

Again:

> *<u>Only</u> I can eat the ritual meal.*
>
> *I can <u>only</u> eat the ritual meal.*
>
> *I can eat <u>only</u> the ritual meal.*

Finally:

> *I can see <u>merely</u> the shadows.*
>
> I can <u>merely</u> see the shadows.

PUNCTUATION, MECHANICS, AND USAGE

Basic Rules and Conventions, Major Errors

This section focuses on the most important and most frequently occurring punctuation and mechanics errors—most important because they have negative effects on the clarity of meaning. Some are repeats and because they are often difficult to identify, the repetition should help you learn to "see" them more readily.

Sentence Fragments (frag) A **sentence fragment** is a group of words wrongly punctuated as if it were a sentence. The group starts with a capital and it ends with a period, question mark, or exclamation point. But it is not a sentence because it lacks one or more of the three ingredients: subject + verb + expression of a complete thought.

Fragments confuse readers who expect a complete thought but who get a partial product causing them to try to "figure it out." Thus, fragments undermine the purpose of writing, clear communication, and they frustrate readers who do not want the burden of puzzle solving.

The most common configuration you will find is illustrated as follows (from a student paper):

> *After everyone takes their* (pn agr) share, I refuse to take treasure; instead, I offer it to my good friend, Gandalf. <u>Which shows how good natured I am</u>*. frag

The underlined fragment (dependent clause) comes after a correct sentence. The fragment expresses a point that is related to the sentence, but it is a dependent clause. Note: dependent clauses are often the most difficult for students to identify because they meet two criteria of a sentence; they have a subject and a verb. They are not, however, complete thoughts.

> **Grammar Highlight:** Reading out loud will frequently make the reader hear the incomplete thought. "*When I get home.*" Hearing that voiced will make the listener say, "When you get home, what?" Encourage students who habitually write fragments to read aloud—not under their breath!

---

*Note this student's pronoun error.

Run-on (fused) Sentences (run) and Comma Splices (cs)

Like the fragment, these errors violate the rules of sentence structure. In this case, it's about connections and misconnections. A railroad analogy helps explain this common error. Imagine that sentences are railroad cars. Now, like them, sentences or separate cars can be linked together—or coupled; they don't have to be separate. Often to get an idea communicated most effectively, as to transport materials across the country, linking is the most effective method. But how?

To begin with, there <u>must</u> be a link. Just as you can't expect to connect by placing two cars next to one another without a coupling mechanism, so, too, the writer cannot simply place two sentences (independent clauses) together without a link, as in:

> *The evening showers were soft and <u>warm they</u> made the night enchanting.*

> *Dublin, king of his breed, strutted as he patrolled his <u>yard his</u> posture blared his dominance through every street and alleyway.*

The underlining identifies where two independent clauses have been fused, or run on, without a coupler. **Note**: in the second example of a run–on sentence, there are two possible ***independent clauses***.

> **Grammar Highlight:** a run–on sentence is not about length; rather it's about structure. A run-on lacks the coupler (FANBOYS, or semi-colon) necessary to link independent clauses.

Comma splice is the second type of fused sentence. Again, it's a problem of connection. You can't link two railroad cars with rubber bands; they are not strong enough. You can't link two independent clauses with a comma—it's not strong enough to do the job of communicating clearly.

> *The evening showers were soft and warm, they made the night enchanting.*

> *Dublin, king of his breed, strutted as he patrolled his yard, his posture blared his dominance through every street and alleyway. cs*

ONLY the FANBOYS or the semi-colon can do the communication job:

The evening showers were soft and warm, and they made the night enchanting.

Dublin, king of his breed, strutted as he patrolled his yard; his posture blared his dominance through every street and alleyway.

Semi-colons are confusing to many students. Yet their correct usage is straightforward and very limited. There are three grammatical situations which require them.

Requirements for a Semi-colon

1	**Compound sentence link:** *"One is not born a woman; one becomes a woman,"* *wrote Simone de Beauvoir.*	**Note** how the semi–colon is selected over the FANBOYS to emphasize the relation between the two independent clauses.
2	**Before a transitional phrase or conjunctive** adverb that comes between two independent clauses, *for instance, therefore, thus, however, as a matter of fact, as a result, for example, in addition, in conclusion, in fact, on the contrary)* *Dr. Holmes tried valiantly to save the ill ferret; however, the bacteria resisted treatment.*	**Note** that a comma comes after the transitional phrase.
3	**To separate items in series with internal punctuation** *The office ordered five boxes of stainless steel, galvanized staples; two cartons of multi-colored, one letter, one legal size; and a gross of pens.*	**Note** commas are usually used to separate items in series except when one of the items (or more) also has a comma.

DON'T	ERROR	REVISION
Do not use to introduce a list or series, or quotation.	There are three points to emphasize; (1) *The king's exact words are; "Total submission."*	There are three points to emphasize: (1) *The king's exact words are: "Total submission."*
Do not use to separate subordinate clause from the main, independent clause of a complex sentence.	*If the weather holds; we will go sailing.* *Finally, he settled down; because the medication was powerful.*	*If the weather holds, we will go sailing.* *Finally, he settled down because the medication was powerful.*
Do not separate appositives with semi-colons.	*Gates; the highest ranking official on the team; spoke well of General Tremor.*	*Gates, the highest ranking official on the team, spoke well of General Tremor.*

Commas

I have spent most of the day putting in a comma and the rest of the day taking it out.

Oscar Wilde

Wilde's wry observation about comma choice highlights two important points: First, and this guides you in editing your and others' writing, that placing commas where they don't belong is a bigger problem with students' writing than failing to use them where they do belong; two, that while we do have rules to guide these decisions, it is often not clear–cut when a comma is necessary.

The uses and misuses of commas are probably the single most troubling punctuation question. Perhaps this is because there are so many situations that require them and also so many situations in which they are incorrectly used. The correct use of commas is crucial to communicating meaning and also to the coherence of writing. Readers are ornery; they don't like to be confused; they do like the sensation of smooth, flowing writing—that's what coherent writing produces.

One guiding principle for all comma use is your best tool. That principle simply is that commas help the reader keep the various parts of a sentence in their proper places. Consider, for instance:

After leaving his friend John made his way to his mother's apartment.

When you read the above sentence, you probably experienced a moment of confusion because your brain connected *friend* to *John*, which is not the meaning of the sentence. Rather:

After leaving his friend, John made his way to his mother's apartment.

Here, the comma helps the reader; it "tells" the reader, "pause to meet *John*, who is the person who left his unnamed friend." As for writing that is incoherent, consider this:

Since Alice hadn't cooked the family decided to dine out.

To which the reader does a double-take: did Alice cook the family? After a confusing moment, the reader may succeed in getting it right—but not without some annoyance. The correctly placed comma avoids the confusion:

Since Alice hadn't cooked, the family decided to dine out.

Now let's look at a different comma problem. Consider: *John took a walk, and talked with Mary about their engagement.* This illustrates a frequently made error: placing a comma to separate a **compound verb**. The comma both breaks the flow of the verb action, putting a brake on the forward movement of *walk* and *talk*, and it confuses the meaning, suggesting that walking and talking are being compared, or that they happened at a different time. It's important to foster this understanding with students.

Comma Dos and Don'ts

Do Use Commas	Don't Use Commas
To separate **introductory clauses** and *phrases* from the main clause: *Since she got her degree, Jeanne has held several challenging positions.* *Traveling at the speed of sound, the jet emits a deafening sonic boom.* *To the extroverts, tourists are a boon; to introverts, they are a curse.* *Having been disappointed in love before, Kate was reluctant to admit that she liked her blind date.*	**Omit** when the dependent clause **follows** the main sentence and a comma pause would interrupt the flow of the statement. *When I was a boy, people were afraid when the stream that ran past the factory didn't change <u>color, because</u> that meant that lay-offs were coming.*
Do Use Commas	**Don't Use Commas**
To separate the independent clauses of a compound sentence linked with a correlative conjunction (FANBOYS) *Dr. Holmes spoke firmly to the distressed client, and she quickly calmed down.*	**Not** after the FANBOYS *Dr. Holmes spoke firmly to the distressed client and, she quickly calmed down. X* **Not** to separate independent clauses *Dr. Holmes spoke firmly to the distressed client, she quickly calmed down. (cs)*
In direct *quotations* separate the subject/speaker from his/her statement: *Dr. Holmes emphatically <u>said, "I will excuse a mischievous pet, but I will not tolerate a bad pet owner."</u>* *"No pets allowed for any reason!" The sign over the entrance says.*	*Be careful not to create a **comma splice**:* *"I don't want to hear about the dunes," I said, "tell me about the experiment."(cs)* *"I dont want to hear about the dunes," I said. "Tell me about the experiment."*
Do use comma for contrasts: *I agree with his facts, not with his interpretations of them.* **Do** use comma after both city and state, or city and country: *In Rome, Italy, we had the best meals of our trip.* *Portland, Oregon's population is twice that of the state.* **Do** use commas with dates and numbers *In December 31, 1775, Washington…*	Do **not** separate compound subjects or compound verbs: *Both the House of Representatives, and the Senate passed the economic stimulus bill.* *Today, both the House and the Senate voted for, and passed the bill.*

Pronouns: Case, Agreement, and Reference

These frequent problems involve the all-important connection between a pronoun and the word to which it refers—its antecedent. As we have previously discussed, confusion in this relationship will obstruct meaning. Pronoun agreement is a very frequent error!

Agreement (agr): Does the pronoun match (agree) the number (singular/plural), gender (male/female), and person (1st, 2nd, 3rd) of its antecedent?

Examples:

> *Athletes frequently suffer injuries to <u>their</u> bodies.*

Athletes, the antecedent is **plural** in number, **neutral** in gender, and in the **third** person. *Their* is plural in number, neutral in gender, and in the third person.

> *A reader must focus his/her attention sharply in order to see the miniscule marks in the margins.*

A reader, the antecedent, is singular in number, either male or female, and in the third person. So, too, are *his* and *her*.

To be inclusive, whenever an antecedent can be either male or female, you need to use both *his* and *her* (so as not to exclude either the female or the male). However, too many of these constructions in a piece of writing make for awkwardness. To avoid these gender constructions often requires creating different sentence formats. For instance, changing the antecedent to plural removes the awkwardness because the plural doesn't have different gender form.

> *Readers must focus their attention sharply in order to see the miniscule marks in the margins.*

Agreement Challenges: Once the basic "mirror relationship" is understood, it seems easy to follow the agreement rule. However, there are several words and grammar constructions which cause difficulties.

Collective nouns—that is, nouns that refer to more than one person such as *team, jury, committee, army*. Note these words are singular in form; they therefore require a singular pronoun as in this example:

The committee left the boardroom and announced its decision to the court.

Sometimes, however, a writer does mean to describe the separate members of a collective and in this case, since the reference is to more than one, then the pronoun should be plural.

The committee left the boardroom and went to their offices to cast their votes for the proposal.

Personal pronouns called indefinites because they don't specify gender or number take the **singular**.

Everyone is responsible for his/her belongings and must take precautions to secure them.

Anybody can apply by submitting his/her qualifications and years of experience.

Each student has his/her own computer.

Every book must be returned with its cover.

Commonly used Indefinite Pronouns

everything	anyone	something	nothing	each
everyone	anything	someone	nobody	every
everybody	anybody	somebody	no one	

Faulty or unclear pronoun reference (ref)

Consider the pronouns in the sentence:

Jane hit the ball so hard that she sent it flying twenty feet over the fence.

We understand this because we clearly understand that the antecedent of *she* is *Jane* and that the antecedent of it is *ball*. This clear relationship is sometimes ambiguous or incorrect.

Claudia threw the vase at the window and broke it.

It is ambiguous; is it the window or the vase that was broken?

The Andersons told the next door neighbors that their children were chasing the chickens.

(Whose children—the neighbors' or the Andersons'?)

Pronoun Case (case)

Subjective case is for pronouns functioning as subjects.

Examples: *She purchased every bottle the store had. (subjective, singular)*

We purchased every bottle the store had. (subjective, plural)

Objective case is for pronouns functioning as objects.

Examples: *They called him from the pay phone. (objective, singular)*

They called us from the pay phone. (objective, plural)

Possessive case is for pronouns functioning to indicate "belonging to."

Examples: *Gloria Gaynor sang her disco hits. (possessive, singular)*

The Bee Gees sang their hits from Saturday Night Fever. (possessive, plural)

Pronoun Case

Pronoun Type	Subjective Case (Nominative)		Objective Case		Possessive Case	
Personal Pronoun	I you he, she, it	we you they	me you him, her, I	us you them	my, mine your his, hers, theirs its	our, ours yours, their
Relative Pronouns	who	whoever	whom	whomever	whose	whosever

When you struggle to decide between using *I* and *me*, or *who* and *whom*, you are grappling with pronoun case. The right answer is in the rules above. However, two situations can make pronoun case difficult. One is because we often violate these rules in speech, so much so that the correct use sounds unnatural or pedantic as in *"Whom did he call?"* Yet, this is correct because *whom* is the object of the verb *call*. Second, there are several grammatical formats that cause confusion and make it tricky to determine whether the case we need is the subjective or the objective. Knowing these confusing formats helps us identify the most common problems people have with pronoun case.

Common Problems with Pronoun Case

Challenging Case Usages	Examples
Compound subjects with a **pronoun** require the **subjective case**.	*Mary and I went shopping together.* ≠ *Mary and me went shopping together.*
Appositives with **pronouns** need to agree with the case of the word they rename.	*The Smiths, both he and she, attended.* ≠ *The Smiths, both him and her, attended.* *They photographed only two actors, the lead man and me.*
The items being compared (*as, as much as, than*) with need to match each other in case.	*I run faster than she (does)* ≠ *I run faster than her.* *The Professor graded us all as hard as (he graded) him.* *We liked nobody else as much as her* *We felt as bad as she.*
A **pronoun** referring back to the subject after a linking verb is in the **subjective case**.	*It was I (≠ me) who rang the bell.* *The principal announced that the essay winners were he and I. (≠ him and me)*
Who and *whom* are problems generally in subordinate clauses or in questions. *Who* or *whom* depends on its function in the subordinate clause that it starts. In questions, usage depends on whether the **pronoun** is the **subject** or the **object** of the question.	*The student (who will address the class) asked for a stipend.* The subordinate clause in the ( ) = *who* (subject of *will address*). *The woman (whom he gave the ring to) is the one he will marry.* *Who got to the finish line first?* *Whom did you recommend for the reward?*
We or *us* before a **noun** is in same case as the noun	*We students want more fairness in grading.* *The supervisor wanted to fire us teenagers.*

Plurals and Possessives

Forming plurals

Most nouns can be singular or plural. The usual plural form adds –s to the end of the word.

desk   desks   book   books

However, there are exceptions to this guideline. After a –y preceded by a consonant, the –y changes to –i and –es is added.

sky   skies   secretary   secretaries

If the final –y is preceded by a vowel, no change is made, and the plural is formed by adding –s.

decoy   decoys   attorney   attorneys

If the last sound in the word is a sibilant—a word ending in –s, –z, –ch, –sh, or –x, or –z—add –es.

churches, sashes, masses, foxes, quizzes (however, with words ending in the sound of –z, it must be doubled before adding the –es)

class   classes

However, if the –ch is pronounced –k, only –s is added.

stomach   stomachs

Often the final –fe or –f in one-syllable words becomes –ves.

half   halves

wife   wives

There are exceptions, of course.

chief	chiefs
roof	roofs

Many nouns have plural forms that are irregular or the same.

child	children	mouse	mice
woman	women	series	series

For nouns ending in *o*, it depends on the word whether you add –*s* or –*es* to form the plural. These spellings must be memorized individually.

potato, potatoes   hero, heroes

Finally, there are a number of foreign words that have become part of the language and retain their foreign plural form. There is a trend to anglicize the spelling of some of these plural forms by adding –*s* to the singular noun. In the list that follows, the letter(s) in parentheses indicate the second acceptable spelling as listed by *Webster's New Collegiate Dictionary*.

datum	data
medium	media
crisis	crises
parenthesis	parentheses
criterion	criteria
phenomenon	phenomena (s)

As you can see, there are many peculiarities associated with plural formation. Keep a dictionary on hand to check plural forms.

Possessive nouns (those that own something, or to which something belongs) use apostrophe plus an *s* (*s'*) as in,

Eleanor Roosevelt's husband was perhaps the most famous president of the twentieth century; or,

The classroom's ceiling is too high to be energy efficient; or,

Charles Manson's behavior has become synonymous with modern psychosocial disorder.

If the noun showing possession is plural, and it ends as most plurals do, with an *–s* (boys, girls, and engineers), then only an apostrophe is used:

The engineers' computers are left on even during the evening when they are not around.

The girls' attitudes made them a delight to work with.

However, there are nouns that do not use an *–s* to form their plural. These non *–s* ending plurals—such as children, men, women—use an apostrophe and an *–s* to show possession:

The women's hats are all different colors.

The children's playground is across the street.

Joint Possession: In situations where two nouns "possess" something together, add the *s* apostrophe (*s'*) to the last noun owner:

John and Mary's Mercedes Benz is frequently borrowed by their son for dates.

Be careful, however, if the subject nouns "own" separate and different things, then each requires an *'s*:

Although they are married, John's and Mary's bank accounts are in different banks.

Possessive Pronouns do not use any form of apostrophe *s*. They are possessive in themselves and require no special sign:

The tree cast its shadow across the field. (Not *it's*, which means *it is*; not *its'*: It's not a word!)

Singular and Plural Possessives

Number		Possessive	
Singular	**Plural**	**Singular possessive**	**Plural possessive**
idea	ideas	*The idea's power,* or *the power of the idea*	*The ideas' power,* or *the power of the ideas*
girl	girls	*The girl's jacket,* or *the jacket of the girl*	*The girls' jackets,* or *the jackets of the girls*
army	armies	*The army's position,* or *the position of the army*	*The armies' positions,* or *the positions of the armies*
class	classes	*The class's objective,* or *the objective of the class*	*The classes' objectives,* or *the objectives of the classes*
child	children	*The child's mind,* or *the mind of the child*	*The children's minds,* or *the minds of the children*
man	men	*The man's thoughts,* or *the thoughts of the man*	*The men's thoughts,* or *the thoughts of the men*
potato	potatoes	*The potato's color,* or *the color of the potato*	*The potatoes' blight,* or *the blight of the potatoes*

Special Uses of Apostrophes

With plural words that end in *s*, add the apostrophe to show possession:

All of the boats' lights shone in the harbor. (the lights of all the boats)

When showing the plural of individual letters of the alphabet, add an apostrophe *s*.

> *John could write his <u>a</u>s perfectly clearly but he had difficulty with his b's.*

Note how the omission of the apostrophe in the lowercase plural for the letter *a* would confuse the reader (is it *as*?).

Contractions use an apostrophe to show that letters have been omitted, frequently in auxiliary verb constructions such as does + not = don't, have + not = *haven't*, and the one often misused as a possessive, it + is = *it's*.

Faulty Predication (fp) occurs when the subject (the 'who' or "what" of the verb) doesn't fit with the predicate:

> *Writing is where I have my greatest problems*. (The subject *writing* is not a place (where)).

> *Horses are the activity she most relishes*. (The subject *horses* is not an activity)

Revision:

> *I have my greatest problems with writing*. Or, *writing is my greatest problem*.

In the second example, note that "my greatest" uses subjective case because it is the complement of a linking verb (to be).

Revision: *Horseback riding is the activity she most relishes.*

When to Use a Colon

Yes	Examples	No!	Incorrect
After salutations	*Dear Mr. Rodriguez:* *Dear Sir:*	Not following the verb *to be*	*Her flaws are: greed, envy, and sloth.*
Before a list introduced by *such as, the following, a number*	*The essay covered the following topics: customs, rituals, play, and dance.* *From the many ideas the professor discussed, she emphasized three: feudal relationships, courtly romance, and knighthood.*	Not following a preposition	*The lecture was about: medicine, surgery, and massage therapy.*
Before a long quotation *Note the capital letter after the colon. This follows APA manual; MLA and CMS do not capitalize	*The Senator emphasized the crisis: "In troubled eras, when tumult and confusion seem normal, and peace, an illusion, great leaders shine like beacons in a dark night."*	Not following a linking verb	*The children's faces seemed: pale, thin, and sharp.*
Between two sentences when the second one explains or re-states the first one	*The truth will set you free: It undoes the shackles on your mind.*		
Dates, titles, ratios, chapter and verse of biblical citations	*Affirmatives outperformed negatives 2:1.* *June: 2007; 1:15; John 5:3* *"The Fictional Detective: A Psychological Study"*		

Quotations and Quotation Marks

Quotation marks are necessary with **direct quotes,** which are words that someone else exactly said or words exactly as they are written or spoken from a source such as a book or film.

> *Mary gave me very precise directions. "Do not," she urged, "enter the kitchen, and do not open the door to the basement."*

> *According to the philosopher, Hannah Arendt, "Evil is banality."*

Indirect quotes are reports on what someone said, summarizing or paraphrasing it. They do not take quotation marks.

> *Sarah said that yesterday had been the worst of her life.*

> *The historian Barbara Tuchman claimed that World War I was an unnecessary mistake.*

Note: the word *that* is generally a sign that you are dealing with an indirect quotation. To indicate someone's exact words, not the writer's, requires quotation marks as when a character in a short story makes a statement:

> *John turned to Mary and confessed, "I quit my job."*

In essays, however, most quotations are to acknowledge another writer's words on the subject of the essay; and in an argumentative/persuasive essay, we often use quotations as evidence to support our arguments.

Quotation Mechanics and Punctuation

Where and when to capitalize, to place quotation marks and punctuation marks such as period, question marks, and exclamation points is largely dependent upon the position of the quotation.

If it is at the beginning, the quotation starts with a capital, and ends with a comma inside the quotation marks. The same is true for question marks and exclamation points.

> *"I have loved you since we were children," Mary admitted to John.*

> *"Did you really love me all along?" John asked. "Yes!" Mary exclaimed.*

If it is at the end of the sentence, place a comma after the source of the quotation, a capital letter for the first word, and the terminal punctuation if a period, question mark, or exclamation point inside the quotation marks.

> *Wendell Phillips says, "The Tree of Liberty requires constant pruning to maintain vital and true."*

The **broken quotation** is a bit more complicated. Let's examine the varieties:

> *"The unexamined life," says Socrates, "is not worth living."*

Note: The beginning follows the same format as noted above. The second part, which is a continuation of the first, is not capitalized, needs a comma after the source, and follows the same rules for placing the period inside the quotation marks. If, however, the quotation consists of two sentences with its source in the middle, note the changes:

> *"The unexamined life is not worth living," says Socrates. "It is the life of the beast, not of the man."*

Quotation marks for titles

Colons and semi-colons go outside of the quotation marks:

> *The document stressed the accident's "special circumstances": It insisted that the holiday atmosphere changed normal behavior.*

> *The killer coldly confessed that he "felt nothing at all"; then, he leaned back in his chair and yawned.*

> **Grammar Highlight:** Commas, periods, question marks and exclamation points are inside the quotation marks; colons and semi-colons are outside of them.

However, there are some tricky situations: Sometimes a quotation is not itself a question or an exclamation, but it's part of a larger sentence that is a question or exclamation. In these cases, the question mark and exclamation point go outside the quotation marks.

Does Mr. Babbitt think he is alone in thinking that new courthouse is "a monument to injustice more than a temple of justice"? (It's not Mr. Babbitt's question.)

Samson didn't have to go so far as to call the defendant "disreputable, heartless scoundrel"! (It's not Samson who is outraged at these words.)

Embedded Quotations: When quotations are part of the larger sentence, note that there are no commas:

I pointed out to Jason that his belief that "all abuse cases should be treated the same" would lead to an abuse in justice.

The Judge concluded that the defendant is "a total psychopath incapable of redemption"; no doubt, his sentence will be harsh and invoke the maximum penalty the law permits.

Ellipses are used to indicate that material has been omitted from a quotation:

The author stated that his work "is meant to entertain, to instruct…but not to preach."

If the omitted material comes in between two sentences in a quotation, add a period:

The author stated that his work "is meant to entertain, to instruct, to promote good values…."

Italics

Word processing has made font styling easier and thus italics have replaced underlining in many instances.

Major use	Example		
Books	*Gone with the Wind*		
Magazines	*Newsweek*	*Wired*	
Plays	*Cats*	*The Glass Menagerie*	
Newspapers	*The Boston Globe*	*The San Francisco Chronicle*	
Ships, planes	*Mayflower*	*The Spirit of St. Louis*	
Films	*The Exorcist*	*Terminator*	
TV shows	*American Idol*	*Lost*	*The Situation Room*
Radio shows	*Democracy Now*		
Music	*Sentimental Journey*		
Art works	*Mona Lisa*	*David*	*Starry Night*
Websites	*Google*	*NYTimes.com*	
Electronic databases	*InfoTrac*		

Italics and their Uses

Italics	Examples	Do not use (common errors)
titles	See list on page 251.	Not with article titles or book chapters. These are indicated with quotation marks. Not to the title of your papers
Words, letters, or numbers that identify themselves not what they commonly mean	To celebrate his invention of the telegraph, Edison named his children *Dot and Dash*. Gerunds are formed by adding *–ing to the verb base;* *Adverbs by adding –y* to an adjective	
Names of specific diseases	*Congestive Heart Failure; Alzheimer's; MS*	Not general disease types: Cancer; paralysis; a fever
Foreign words	I was *enchante* to have made his acquaintance.	Foreign words that have become part of English: laissez-faire economics; or potpourri

CAPITALIZATION

 A very important element of writing is knowing when to capitalize a word and when to leave it alone. When a word is capitalized, it calls attention to itself. This attention should be for a good reason. There are standard uses for capital letters. In general, capitalize (1) all proper nouns, (2) the first word of a sentence, and (3) the first word of a direct quotation. The following lists outline specific guidelines for capitalization.

What Should Be Capitalized

Capitalize the names of ships, aircraft, spacecraft, and trains:

Apollo 13

Boeing 767

DC–10

HMS *Bounty*

Mariner 4

Sputnik II

Capitalize the names of divine beings:

God

Allah

Buddha

Holy Ghost

Jehovah

Jupiter

Shiva

Venus

Capitalize the geological periods:

Cenozoic era

Neolithic age

Ice Age

late Pleistocene times

Capitalize the names of astronomical bodies:

Big Dipper

Halley's comet

Mercury

the Milky Way

North Star

Ursa Major

Capitalize personifications:

Reliable Nature brought her promised Spring.

Bring on Melancholy in his sad might.

She believed that Love was the answer to all her problems.

Capitalize historical periods:

Age of Louis XIV

Christian Era

the Great Depression

the Middle Ages

Reign of Terror

the Renaissance

Roaring Twenties

World War I

Capitalize the names of organizations, associations, and institutions:

Common Market

Franklin Glen High School

Girl Scouts

Harvard University

Kiwanis Club

League of Women Voters

Library of Congress

New York Philharmonic

Pittsburgh Steelers

North Atlantic Treaty Organization

Smithsonian Institution

Unitarian Church

Capitalize government and judicial groups:

Arkansas Supreme Court

British Parliament

Committee on Foreign Affairs

Department of State

Georgetown City Council

Peace Corps

U.S. Census Bureau

U.S. Court of Appeals

U.S. House of Representatives

U.S. Senate

A general term that accompanies a specific name is capitalized only if it follows the specific name. If it stands alone, comes before the specific name, or is used on second reference, it is lowercased:

Central Park, the park

Golden Gate Bridge, the bridge

the Mississippi River, the river

Monroe Doctrine, the doctrine of expansion

President Obama, the president of the United States

Pope Benedict XVI, the pope

Queen Elizabeth I, the queen of England

Senator Dixon, the senator from Illinois

Treaty of Versailles, the treaty

Tropic of Capricorn, the tropics

Webster's Dictionary, the dictionary

Washington State, the state of Washington

Capitalize the first word of a sentence:

Our car would not start.

When will you leave? I need to know right away.

Never!

Let me in! Please!

When a sentence appears within a sentence, start it with a capital letter:

We had only one concern, "When would we eat?"

My sister said, "I'll find the Monopoly game."

He answered, "We can only stay a few minutes."

The most important words of titles are capitalized. Those words not capitalized are conjunctions (*and, or, but*) and short prepositions (*of, on, by, for*). The first and last word of a title must always be capitalized:

A Man for All Seasons

Crime and Punishment

Of Mice and Men

Rise of the West

Strange Life of Ivan Osokin

Sonata in G Minor

"Let Me In"

"Ode to Billy Joe"

Rubaiyat of Omar Khayyam

All in the Family

Capitalize newspaper and magazine names:

> *The New York Times*
>
> *the Washington Post*
>
> *National Geographic*
>
> *U.S. News & World Report*

Capitalize radio and TV network abbreviations or station call letters:

> ABC
>
> CNN
>
> HBO
>
> NBC
>
> WBOP
>
> WNEW

Capitalize regions:

> the Northeast, the South, the West
>
> Eastern Europe
>
> but: the south of France, the east side of town

Capitalize specific military units:

> the U.S. Army, but: the army, the German navy, the British air force
>
> the Seventh Fleet
>
> the First Infantry Division

Capitalize political organizations, and in some cases, their philosophies, and members:

> Democratic Party, the Communist Party
>
> Marxist
>
> Whigs

Nazism

Federalist (in U.S. history contexts)

But do not capitalize systems of government or individual adherents to a philosophy:

democracy, communism

fascist, agnostic

Do not capitalize compass directions or seasons:

north, south, east, west

spring, summer, winter, autumn

Capitalize specific diseases:

Alzheimer's

Swine Flu

DON'T capitalize general diseases:

cancer

flu

heart disease

Capitalize search engines, names of computer programs, internet service providers, websites, electronic databases:

Google

Yahoo

Microsoft Word

America Online

HotWired

LexisNexis

InfoTrak

Numbers, the basics

When to spell out a number and when to use the numeral (ten, or 10)—that's the question! Unfortunately, there's no simple answer because the experts differ: some say spell out numbers between one and ten, and use numerals for all above ten: *Only 59 students out of 100 passed the test*. Some experts, however, recommend spelling out all the numbers from one to ninety-nine. So chose whichever you like best, but be consistent.

There are some clear cut guidelines however. Never begin a sentence with a number—it must be spelled out:

> **CORRECT:** *Fifty-nine out of 100 students passed the test.*

> **INCORRECT:** *20 students flunked the exam.*

Do not spell, rather use numbers for any requiring more than two words:

> **CORRECT:** *We sent out 157 invitations.*

> **INCORRECT:** *We sent out one hundred fifty-seven invitations.*

If two numbers are next to one another, spell out one and use a number for the other:

> **CORRECT:** *John ran three, 50 yard races.*

> **INCORRECT:** *John ran 3, 50 yard races.*

Percentages, statistics, distances, money are not spelled out, unless they begin a sentence!

> **CORRECT:** *Recycling removes 25% of waste from landfills.*

> **INCORRECT** *25% of the population recycles.*

> **CORRECT:** *Twenty-five percent of the population recycles.*

> **CORRECT:** *We drove 10 miles out of the way to find a Starbucks.*

> **CORRECT:** *The sweater cost $59.99.*

Commonly Misused Words and Phrases

Note that many of the confusions involve parts of speech.

A lot/a lot: *a lot* is informally used a lot. But it is incorrect.

> *"A lot" is a much used informal phrase; do not use it in your writing.*

Advice/advise: advice is a noun; advise, a verb.

> *I never asked for your advice.*

> *The counselor advised me to research the biotechnology field.*

Affect/effect: *affect* is a verb meaning "to influence, or have impact upon"; *effect* is a noun meaning results of; *effect* can also be used to mean influence, or impact but not as a verb: The effects of nuclear radiation are radiation sickness, soil contamination, and global pollution.

> *Poverty affects the incidence of animal neglect. When people are short on cash, they sometimes abandon their pets.*

> *My paper concerns the effects of television violence on children's behavior.*

All ready/already: *all ready* means fully prepared; *already* is an adverb meaning previously or before.

> *I was all ready to leave for my trip when I got the surprise cancellation.*

> *By the time I arrived home, the family had already eaten.*

Bad/badly: *bad* is an adjective and thus modifies nouns and pronouns; *badly* is an adverb.

> *John looked bad after his accident*

> *John was badly hurt in the accident.*

Breath/breathe: *Breath* is a noun; *breathe* is a verb.

> *I was all out of breath by the time I reached the summit.*

> *She was so frightened that she couldn't breathe.*

Capitol/capital: A *capitol* is a building wherein a legislative body meets. A *capital* is either a political center as in, *Boston is the capital of Massachusetts*, or it refers to the uppercase letter that must begin all sentences. Capital can also mean goods, assets, cash.

> *Madoff bilked many investors of their capital.*

Complement/compliment: *complement* means to go along with, to match; *compliment* means "to flatter." Both can be either nouns or verbs.

> *The professor complimented the class on its stellar performance.*

> *As one of the class members, I felt honored by his compliment.*

Conscience: the part of mind that experiences right and wrong

> *After lying to his girlfriend, Jim's conscience bothered him.*

Conscientious: an adjective meaning very careful, attentive to requirements

> *He is a very conscientious teacher; lectures are always well-prepared.*

Conscious: an adjective meaning aware or deliberate

> *Irena is often not conscious of how alienating her behavior can be.*

Continual/continuous: *continuous* refers to something that never stops; *continual* to something that happens frequently but not always.

> *The continuous force of evolution means that change is inevitable.*

> *Rainfall is the result of the continuous cycle of evaporation and condensation linking the waters of the earth and the clouds of its atmosphere.*

> *The college students in the apartment above us have frequent parties that continually disturb us in the middle of the night.*

Council/counsel: *council* is a noun and signifies a group; *counsel* is either a noun or a verb meaning advice or to advise

> *Four magnificent mutts, Dublin, Logan, Molly, and Sasha elected me to the Council of All Beings.*

> *The council debated heatedly before finally deciding to whom the prize was awarded.*

> *The therapist counseled my best friend to leave her relationship.*

> *When I met her partner, I gave her the same counsel.*

Desert/dessert: *desert* is an arid land; *dessert* is a delicious sweet food.

> *Arizona contains many deserts.*

> *Dessert is the best part of the meal.*

> *Mnemonics: As a desert lacks water, so the word lacks an s.*

Every day/everyday: *every day* is a phrase, two words meaning "happening daily"; *everyday,* one word, meaning ordinary, usual

> *Every day I go to the gym to work out.*

> *Arguments at dinner are everyday affairs.*

Farther/further: *farther* refers to physical distance, while *further* refers to difference in degree or time

> *The restaurant is about two miles farther down this road.*
>
> *His shifting eyes were further proof of guilt.*

Good/well: *good* is an adjective; *well* is an adverb. Hence,

> *I may look good, but I don't feel well.*
>
> *He cooks very well.*

Hanged/hung: unless you are referring to stringing someone up by a rope, use *hung*.

> *The stockings were hung on the chimney. The clothes hung on the line.*
>
> *The vigilantes hanged John Dooley for his thievery.*

Its/it's: *its* is a possessive form of *it*—a pronoun; *it's* a contraction of *it is*.

> *Our town must improve its roads.*
>
> *It's time to leave the zoo.*

Like/as: *like* is a preposition; *as* is a conjunction that introduces a clause. Hence, if a statement has a verb, use *as*; if not, use *like*.

> *Dorothy drank as heartily as a thirsty camel.*
>
> *Her muscles were strong and ropey like a weight lifter's.*

Loose/lose: *loose* means "not attached," the opposite of tight; *lose* means to misplace

> *He has been accused of having loose lips: don't trust him!*
>
> *If I lose these keys, I'll be in serious trouble.*

Passed/past: *passed* is the past tense of the verb, *to pass,* meaning to move by, or succeed; *past* is a noun meaning before the present time

> *We passed two hitchhikers on Route 22.*

> *In times past, people enjoyed much richer social lives.*

Principal/principle: *principal* means a supervisor or something of major importance; *principle* refers to a value, an idea.

> *The principal of Sunnyside High was fired for fiscal irresponsibility. Some pal!*

> *The fired principal was evidently not a man of high principles.*

Proceed, proceeds, precede: *proceed* is a verb meaning to carry on, to go forth; *proceeds*, a plural noun, meaning revenue raised; *precede* is a verb, meaning to be ahead or in front of, or earlier than:

> *"Proceed, counselor," bellowed the judge, "or be fined for stalling."*

> *In the Easter procession, the Bishops, priests, and other clergy precede the parishioners.*

> *The proceeds from the raffle are going to the Food Bank.*

Quote/quotation: *quote* is a verb; *quotation* is a noun

> *I chose a quotation from Karl Marx to summarize the negative effects of capitalism upon family ties.*

> *I quoted Karl Marx to emphasize the adverse effects of capitalism on family ties.*

Raise/rise: *raise* means to elevate, or to increase. Past tense is regular, *raised*; *rise* means to stand up, to get up. Past tense is irregular *rose.*

> *The State Department of Education is charged with raising academic standards.*

> *The reform effort has successfully raised student achievement.*

"All rise for the benediction," the minister directed.

The congregation rose for the benediction as surely as the sun rises every day.

Real/really: *real* is an adjective; *really*, an adverb.

He is a real artist, in my opinion, contrary to the hacks employed in advertising.

He is a really good artist, despite his large commercial appeal.

Set/sit: *set* means to put down or to adjust; its past tense is also *set*. *Sit* is a verb meaning to place oneself in a sitting position; the past is *sat*.

John set his hat on the bureau.

After setting his hat on the bureau, John sat in his favorite chair.

Than/then: *than* is a comparison word; *then* is an adverb referring to time

The politics of health care are more complicated even than those of public education.

I got up at 8:00 AM and, then, five minutes later, I was on my way to the office.

Their/they're: *their* is a possessive pronoun; *there're* is a contraction for *they are*.

The Smiths can be annoying; they're always late for dinner.

Their habitual lateness annoys their friends.

Used to/use to: *used to* is the past tense phrase to express a former action/state; *use to* is simply incorrect.

When American artists migrated to France in the 1920s, they used to gather at the Café Metro in Paris.

Who/whom: *who* is the nominative case; *whom*, the objective case (Review pronoun section)

> *The first person who reaches the goal post wins the prize.*

> *Ask not for whom the bell tolls: It tolls for thee.*

Who's/whose: *who's* is a contraction of *who is*; *whose* is a possessive pronoun

> *The student who's voted the most likely to succeed wins a full scholarship.*

> *The student whose GPA is the highest wins a full scholarship for graduate school.*

Your /you're: *you're* is a contraction of *you are*; *your* is a possessive pronoun

> *The neighbors dislike that you're an environmentalist who doesn't cultivate a lawn.*

> *The neighbors dislike your choice of herbs and stones for your front yard.*

> **Learning Tip:** Mnemonics is an effective tool to help you with confusing words and spelling problems. Making up ways to remember can be entertaining and instructive. For instance, remember that *principal* is a pal (person).

SPELLING

Many of the easily confused words we study are different in spelling such as, **advice/advise**. Many stem from confusing phonetics (how a word sounds) with how it is spelled, a real problem since English contains many words spelled very differently from how they sound. There are some rules to help us. For instance, the jingle that many of us learned:

> *I before e except after c, or when it sounds like "ay" as in neighbor, eighteen, weigh.*

Unfortunately, there are exceptions such as *seize*, *leisure*, *height*.

Plural formations are another area in which some general rules help:

Recall from the section about nouns that most nouns form plural by adding *s*: (flower/ flowers; car/cars). However, if a noun ends in a *–y* that follows a consonant (country), then drop the *y* and substitute *ies*, as in *country/countries* or *story/stories*. However, the *y* is kept if it follows a vowel (*day/days*), or if it ends a proper noun (*Barney/Barneys*).

What's a person to do? Given the many exceptions that characterize English, here are two practical strategies:

- Do not rely on spell-check alone for there are some words it simply cannot pick up.

- Familiarize yourself with the typical problem situations (such as *ie/ei*), pay attention to them, look them up in a dictionary if you are not sure. The following are common words prone to spelling errors:

> *Occurred*
>
> *Heroes*
>
> *Parallel*
>
> *Laboratory*
>
> *Preferred*
>
> *Preference*
>
> *Grievance*

PRACTICE EXERCISES

1. Put a double line under the sentence's main (independent) clause; put a single line under its dependent (subordinate) clause.

   While the writer wanted to create a sense of mystery, he did not succeed.

2. Working with the sentence below, construct two compound sentences using two different connectors.

   Since the day had turned cold and rainy, we decided to skip our walk and to go to a movie instead.

3. Underline all the prepositional phrases in the sentence below. What type of sentence is it?

   To her great disappointment, Sarah did not get into the school of her choice, but to her credit, she immediately reapplied for admission to next year's class.

4. Name the underlined group below. What part of speech is it functioning as?

   Seeing you so upset was disturbing to me.

5. Double underline the 2 main (independent) clauses; single-underline the dependent clause. What type of sentence is this?

   The car that Jack sells gets forty miles per gallon, and it costs under $20,000.

6. Double underline the main (independent) clauses; single-underline the two dependent clauses. What sentence type is this?

   Except that she is overweight, Sandra met all the physical requirements for the firefighters' union, although that one problem may keep her out.

7. Both of these sentences have the same problem. What is it? Construct two sentences that correct the problem.

    Jeff wants either to go to college or a cross-country trip. If he takes the trip, he plans to take his dog, his father's RV, and to camp in National Parks.

8. Underline the main (independent) clause in the sentence below. What type of sentence is this?

    In their parents' absence, Tim and John have had to clean house and cook dinner every night for the past two weeks.

9. The sentence below is a(n)

    A. compound sentence.

    B. complex sentence.

    C. simple sentence.

    D. absolute phrase.

    The truck in the backyard is filled with rickety furniture and rusty appliances.

10. The following describes or shows the correct punctuation of the sentence below.

    A. place a comma before *but*.

    B. place a comma before and after *but*.

    C. place commas around *into the evening*.

    D. do nothing; it's correct as it is.

    Sarah studied long into the evening every night for a week but she still failed the test.

11. The underlined section of the sentence below is a(n)

    A. independent clause.

    B. prepositional phrase.

    C. dependent clause.

    D. appositive phrase.

    After the dust settled and feelings were calmed, *we could speak logically and resolve our differences.*

12. The three criteria for a sentence are

    I.   a subject
    II. a verb
    III. an independent clause
    IV. a complete thought
    V.   a predicate
    VI. a direct object

    A. I, III, VI

    B. II, VI, V

    C. I, II, IV

    D. V, VI, II

13. Which of the following statements is most accurate?

    A. A fragment is a phrase that is not a complete thought.

    B. A fragment is a dependent clause incorrectly punctuated with a beginning capital and an ending period.

    C. A fragment is a dependent clause attached to an independent clause.

    D. A fragment is two or more clauses incorrectly connected to one another.

14. The underlined phrase in the sentence below is most fully described by as a

    A. modifier of *difficulty*.

    B. prepositional phrase with a gerund functioning as an adverb modifying *difficulty*.

    C. prepositional phrase with a verb that modifies the adverb, *difficulty*.

    D. gerund functioning as an indirect object.

Leonardo da Vinci could paint exquisitely, but he had great difficulty <u>with writing</u>.

15. Which of the following statements BEST describes the sentence below?

    A. It is a well-constructed complex sentence.

    B. It is a sentence beginning with a participial phrase that is correctly punctuated with a comma.

    C. It is a sentence with a dangling modifier.

    D. It is a simple sentence with a gerund phrase.

Failing to pass the test, all the potential benefits were lost.

16. Which of the following **BEST** describes the sentence below?

    A. The sentence opens with a misplaced modifier and needs to be revised.

    B. The sentence opens with a dependent clause, is attached to an independent clause, and is a complex one.

    C. This is a compound sentence incorrectly punctuated with a comma.

    D. This is a simple sentence that contains two gerunds.

Hiding in the dark shadows cast by the trees, the searchers had a difficult time seeing the wandering livestock.

Practice Exercise Answers

1. *While the writer wanted to create a sense of mystery, he did not succeed.*

2. *The day had turned cold and rainy, so we decided to skip our walk and to go to a movie.*

   The day had turned cold and rainy; therefore, we decided to skip our walk and to go to a movie.

3. *To her great disappointment, Sarah did not get into the school of her choice, but to her credit, she immediately re-applied for admission to next year's class.*

   Compound sentence connected with one of the FANBOYS.

4. *Seeing you so upset was disturbing to me.*

   1. gerund phrase

   2. noun (subject of the verb *was*)

5. *The car that Jack sells gets forty miles per gallon, and it costs under $20,000.*

   The car that Jack sells gets forty miles per gallon, and it costs under $20,000.

6. *Except that she is overweight, Sandra met all the physical requirements for the firefighters' union, although that one problem may keep her out.*

   Complex sentence

7. Both are weakened by lack of parallel structures

   Jeff wants either to go to college or to take a cross-country trip. *If he takes the trip, he plans to take his dog, to drive his father's RV, and to camp in National Parks.*

8. *In their parents' absence, Tim and John have had to clean house and cook dinner every night for the past two weeks.*

   Simple Sentence

9. **C**   Simple sentence with only one independent clause.

10. *Sarah studied long into the evening every night for a week but she still failed the test.*

    A   Comma always comes before a FANBOYS in a compound sentence.

11. C   A dependent clause since *we could speak logically and resolve our differences* makes no sense on its own.

12. C   A sentence requires a subject, verb, and a complete thought.

13. B   Since a phrase can be a complete thought (A) is not correct. And both (C) and (D) are not necessarily true, (B) is the correct answer.

14. B   (B) is the only possible answer.

15. B   It is a sentence beginning with a participial phrase that is correctly punctuated with a comma.

16. A   The sentence opens with a misplaced modifier and needs to be revised.

INDEX

NOTES

NOTES

NOTES

NOTES